TYCOONS

ORIGINAL OBITUARIES OF 50 PIONEERS OF BUSINESS

BLUE MAGPIE BOOKS

Blue Magpie

CONTENTS

RICHARD ARKWRIGHT JR (DECEMBER 19, 1755 – APRIL 23, 1843)

THE MANCHESTER GUARDIAN, MAY 3, 1843

*W*e have already announced the demise of this gentleman, and we obtain the following particulars connected with the accumulation of his vast property from *The Morning Herald*. He died possessed, it is reported, of not less than seven millions sterling in personal property alone, irrespective of landed estates.

As an individual capitalist, there is not one in Europe at the present time who can approach within half the distance, excepting, perhaps, the excellent no less than wealthy Mr Solomon Heine, of Hamburg, who, according to general repute, is estimated to concentrate in his own person the representation of money values to the vast amount of four millions sterling. It must be remembered, however, that this sum represents the whole property of Mr Heine, whereas the late Mr Arkwright was possessed of landed estates perhaps one or two millions beyond the amount at which the personality is rated.

Immensely wealthy as are the Barings, the Rothschilds, the Hopes, etc, of Europe, there is not, has not been, one that could be placed at all in the comparison: not all the magnificent fortunes drawn out of, with all the vast capital remaining still in, the princely house of Baring would, perhaps, all combined reach to the amount: not all the splendid capitals of all the Rothschilds throughout Europe together equal probably more than one-half the enormous mass of accumulated hordes left behind by the late Mr Arkwright.

Out of Europe, the only capitalist who could approach the comparison would be Mr John Jacob Astor, of New York, whose name will be familiar with all travellers from the massive and magnificent pile of buildings which, as Astor's Hotel has administered to their convenience - a building which, of the description, and for the special use, stands unparalleled in the whole world: with this palatial structure, it must be understood that Mr Astor neither was nor is otherwise connected than as planner and proprietor, and as forming part of his vast estate. The reports current about the enormous wealth created and accumulated by this extraordinary man carry it as high as 16 or 17 millions of dollars, or say about four millions sterling; but of course whilst he is living this can only be matter of conjecture, though perhaps not far from the truth. In illustration of the fact, however, a curious anecdote has been in circulation in the United States.

During the lifetime of the late Stephen Girard, who from a poor outcast exile from San Domingo driven out by the former slave population became the great banker and capitalist of Philadelphia, it was a subject of something like rival contention between the people of Philadelphia and New York which possessed the greatest capitalist - that is, which was the more wealthy man, Girard or Astor. Doubtless the question was not without its interest to the money-making parties themselves. The death of one or the other, or of both, could however alone solve the speculations, and in the former case then only to the survivor. Accordingly, on the death of Stephen Girard, some years ago, the actual extent of his wealth was verified by the publication of his testament, by which the largest proportion was bequeathed for the establishment and support of literary and public institutions. When Mr Astor was informed that the total sum of Girard's wealth reached only to some 11 or 12 millions of dollars, he is reported to have exhibited signs of satisfaction, and in an undertone, as if speaking to himself, to have remarked "that would not do" - meaning of course that it did not come up to the mark of his own prodigious possessions.

The late Mr Richard Arkwright was the only son of Sir Richard Arkwright, the founder and father of the "factory system" as it now exists. He succeeded to all the possessions and numerous spinning factories, on the death of Sir Richard in 1792, then estimated at the value, capital stock included, of about half a million sterling. As the profit of cotton spinning then, and for years afterwards, were counted by shillings per pound, instead of by farthings as now, except in the finer counts, it may be safely asserted that by his extensive spinneries in Cranford, Bakewell and Manchester alone, he should not have derived a less clear income than £100,000 per annum.

The extensive works at Manchester he disposed of some time afterwards in favour of his managers, Messrs Barton and Simpson, who both realised large fortunes. He gave up the spinning works at Bakewell some five or six years ago only to parties who, it is believed, had been long in his service; but those at Cranford, near his own residence, he carried on, as understood, to the time of his death. Mr Richard Arkwright, besides various other concerns highly prosperous for the most part, was the principal if not sole proprietor of some banking establishments in the counties of Derby and Nottingham.

From taste and not from niggardly notions of saving, he lived without the least ostentatious display; the scale of his household expenditure is supposed not to have exceeded £3,000 per annum, of which the larger portion was laid out upon his gardens, on which he prided himself; so that, by the natural and equable force of accumulation, during 52 years, even had not one pound of surplus income been rein-vested and made to bear interest, he must still have been possessed of millions.

He was probably the last of the historic figures connected and coeval with the foundation of what are now designated the factory and power systems. Robert Peel, who may be esteemed the head if not the parent of calico print-ing, realised and bequeathed a vast fortune to his descen-dents. The mountain of wealth accumulated by Mr Arkwright has already been referred to. But James Harg-reaves, the inventor of the "spinning jenny", died in but middling circumstances. Samuel Crompton, the inventor of the "mule" frame, which has carried the art of spinning to its greatest perfection, died in poverty, notwithstanding a parliamentary grant of £5,000, in 1812, which melted away through the misfortunes of his sons in the business in which, by means of this grant, he established them. And, lastly, the late Mr William Radcliffe, of Stockport (whose death occurred only last year), the inventor of the "dressing machines", and veritable father of the "power-loom" system, for before the epoch of that invention the power-loom was powerless and impracticable, perished in almost abject poverty; a fact reflecting no small discredit on the opulent manufacturers of Manchester, who, after plundering him of his invention by the unscrupulous appropriation of which they enriched themselves, might surely have let fall a few crumbs from their own overloaded tables to comfort the old age and penury of the man they contributed to sink into pauperism.

Nor indeed is such a melancholy fact more creditable to a great nation, or a government wielding its destinies. The board of trade, or the treasury did, indeed - we record the fact with the deepest feelings of sorrow and shame - at the last moment, through some indirect application, some member of parliament, it is reported, award the beggarly sum of one hundred and fifty pounds, once told, not even annual, an acknowledgment, in first, full and final acquittance. Of the deserts and claims of a man whose inventions, fruits of the unremitting application of the labour, ingenuity and outlay of consecutive years have enriched the capital of the country with scores, if not hundreds, of millions, and afforded employment to hundreds of thousands of an industrious population. Fast progressing towards his eightieth year, and borne down by age, misfortunes and infirmity, when the intelligence of this munificent token of national remembrance was broken to him it proved too much for the suffering old man; it was like mockery upon misery; and so poor Mr Radcliffe drew his last breath, on the very day, it is said, but if not within one or two days after; the one hundred and fifty pounds came opportunely and mercifully to provide a coffin and gravestone for the dead, and save from the scandal of a parish pauper burial - "he asked for bread; they gave him a stone".

He was a real inventor, and of an original mechanical genius. Wonderful as was the sagacity and enterprise of Sir Richard Arkwright, and extraordinary as the improvements he affected in the inventions of others, he was, in respect of inventions, but "the gatherer and disposer of other men's stuff". The report of the great and final trial in respect of his patents in 1785, the folio edition of which is now before us, establishes the fact. That great trial, it may be remarked, is the foundation of the "patent" law of this country as it now exists.

JOHN JACOB ASTOR (JULY 17, 1763 - MARCH 29, 1848

BROOKLYN DAILY EAGLE, MARCH 30, 1848

*J*ohn Jacob Astor, long celebrated all over the world as the richest man in America, died yesterday morning a little after 9 o'clock, at his residence in New York. He was born in Waldorf, near Heidelberg, in the Grand Duchy of Baden, Germany, in July 1763, and had consequently almost reached the great age of four score and five years. He came to this country in 1783, by the earnest request of a brother, a butcher, who had preceded him hither, and made such representations as finally prevailed.

He was then poor, but soon begun to mend his fortunes, and continued to grow rich until he became much the richest man in the new world. He leaves several children. William Backhouse Astor married the daughter of General John Armstrong, who was Secretary of War under the James Madison administration, and who will inherit the largest part of his father's immense estate. His other son is said to be insane or imbecile. One of his daughters [Eliza] married Count Vincent Rumpff, minister at Paris from the Hanseatic league, and was distinguished for her Christian benevolence. She was engaged in every good work, but has been dead several years. Another daughter [Dorothea] married Mr Walter Langdon of New Hampshire, now in Europe, and a third [Magdalena] the Rev Mr (John) Bristed.

Mr Astor was a man of some ability, but would not have been at all distinguished but for his great wealth.

CORNELIUS VANDERBILT (MAY 27, 1794 – JANUARY 4, 1877)

THE BOSTON DAILY GLOBE, JANUARY 5, 1877

*T*he death of the great railway king has at length occurred. The tenacity of life exhibited by the veteran capitalist made it appear not impossible that his imperial energy and determination would be too much for the King of Terrors. But as the old Duchess of Marlborough, who solemnly declared that she wouldn't die, had to give in at last, so Vanderbilt has finally met the fate which he so long kept off by the vigor of a splendid constitution and the strength of an indomitable will.

Of the three gigantic capitalists of this country and this generation, of whom at his death he was the sole survivor, the doughty Commodore was unquestionably the ablest, the most comprehensive in the extent of his enterprises, and the most vigorous and far reaching in the methods of their execution. William B. Astor, as the London *Spectator* aptly called him, was only a "beaver capitalist" at best, plodding and shrewd within safe and narrow limits. Even the Irish entrepreneur A.T. Stewart was a great shopkeeper, rather than a great merchant, conducting business on a large scale in the spirit and with the traditions of a small one. Neither of these two men wielded the power of Vanderbilt, whose operations were coincident with the development of the resources of the country by those twin brothers of modern enterprise, the steamboat and the railway.

Indeed, not one, but two continents were subsidized by the great magician who held these genii under his control. The Atlantic and Pacific were bridged by his sagacity, and in the pursuance of his projects he made even territorial rulers his tools and victims. A memorable instance of this was afforded by the way in which he fought and overcame the filibuster William Walker in 1856, who was the ruling in Nicaragua. Vanderbilt had then got control of the Transit Company, and when Walker seized its property, the Commodore, bringing to bear the power of Costa Rica on his behalf, fomented an insurrection which hurled from his government the ambitious filibuster who sought to thwart the plans of the steamship king.

Vanderbilt's birth in 1794 occurred at a time when the industrial future of the country was yet undreamed of. The old farmhouse on Staten Island, on the memorable 27th of May in that year, brought to view the individual who was to develop the latent possibilities of our civilization through the agency of steam. New York then contained only 80,000 inhabitants, and the father of Cornelius Vanderbilt was a boatman, who, from a thriving farmer carrying his own and others' produce to market, became in this humble way the founder of the Staten Island ferry. He was fortunate in the possession of a wife who saved him from the ruin which his imprudence in business enterprises once threatened him with, and the fact that she left at her death, at the great age of 87, an estate of $50,000, the fruit of her own careful industry, attests her substantial merits. We have the authority of Mr James Parton, the Commodore's trusted biographer, for saying that Vanderbilt loved to acknowledge that whatever he had, and whatever he was that is good, he owed to the precepts, the example, and the judicious government of his mother.

The eldest of a family of nine children, the future steamboat and railway king had few advantages for schooling, but his love for outdoor exercises and passionate fondness for horses were shown at a very early age. At 16, he owned a boat, bought with his own earnings, and he soon became the best boatman in the port. Vanderbilt's sagacity in forecasting the changes in modes of transportation, which has been the secret of his success, led him in 1818, when he was only 24 years old, to sell out his trim sailing vessels and become the captain of a small steamboat. How after 12 years of service in this capacity he saved 12,000 dollars and set up for himself became chiefly interesting from the fact that, during his steamboat career, he owned no less than 21 steamers, 11 of which he built, and with steamboats his entire steam fleet numbered 66. This extensive connection with the steamship business gave him the title of Commodore. In 1864, he abandoned the water entirely, and as he had 47 years before discerned the supremacy of steam over sails, so this last step was an illustration of his prescience, which had for a long time beheld the paramount importance of railways.

As early as 1844, Vanderbilt had become a large owner in the New York and New Haven Railroad, and in 1845 began to buy Harlem, the entire stock of which he held in 1864. The price of its shares was low in 1861, and the subsequent advance, owing to the action of the New York Common Council two years later, in his favor, occasioned short sales in expectation of a reconsideration. The Commodore then cornered the stock, raising it from about 78 or 79 to 220, squeezing the bears and enriching himself and his friends by the operation.

In 1859, and subsequently, he invested several millions in the mortgage bonds of the Erie Railroad. The acquisition of Harlem led to Vanderbilt's purchase of a controlling interest in the Hudson River and New York Central, which he consolidated, and since 1873 the Michigan Southern road has been operated in conjunction with them as one continuous route 978 miles in extent, and with Harlem and side lines and branches, making an aggregate of 2,128 miles under one management, and representing an aggregate capital of 149 millions, one-half of which is said to be controlled by the Vanderbilt family.

The Commodore's recent action in fighting the Baltimore and Ohio and other roads in the interest of New York is too familiar to require more than a passing mention. It should be said, in justice to Vanderbilt, who has too often been confounded with mere stock speculators, that his primary object in buying railroads was to improve them. Thus, he converted Harlem and Hudson from the footballs of the Stock Exchange into sound dividend-paying investments, and the New York Central, notwithstanding the extensive watering of its stock, represents a value today which is mainly owing to his skilful, sagacious management.

Between such a stock gambler as the steamship and railroad tycoon Daniel Drew and the Commodore there was really nothing in common, except a certain unscrupulousness as to the choice of means in attaining a desired end. We do not lay much stress on the Commodore's benevolence, and his gift of 700,000 dollars to Nashville University, 300,000 to remain as a permanent invested endowment, was doubtless made like Drew's benefactions to Methodist institutions, as a sop to public opinion. Personally, the

Commodore's tastes, except in the matter of horseflesh, were simple. His superb steam yacht North Star, in which he went to Europe, was a solitary piece of extravagance, and when he gave a great steamer to the Government in war times he doubtless felt as every large property owner did, that self interest required some sacrifices to the cause of country.

Vanderbilt's untiring devotion to business in business hours was doubtless one secret of his success, which he himself said was due to the fact that he never told what he was going to do till be had done it. Like most men of action he was no speechmaker, though he could talk well on subjects on which he was interested. He was not scholarly in his tastes, and preferred playing whist and point-euchre with his cronies to more intellectual diversions. The uncontern with which he heard of Robert Schuyler's defalcations, while at his favorite game at Saratoga, showed that he did not allow business troubles to follow him to his recreations. To this regulation of his mind and body was due his prolonged good health, and his taste for fast horses, which in him could hardly be called an extravagance, tended to the same end, by keeping him in the open air.

While everyone must recognize in the deceased railway king a great power in the practical life of the country, it would be absurd to claim for him the honors of the philanthropist, the statesman, or the self-sacrificing patriot. He was great within his range, and it may be counted his misfortune and not his fault, considering the defects of his early training, that there were not more refining and elevating influences in his long, active and, on the whole, useful life.

The New York Times, January 5, 1877

WHEN CORNELIUS VANDERBILT became 16 years of age, he bargained with his mother that he would plow eight acres of the farm and plant it with corn if she would give him $100 for the purchase of a boat. It is unnecessary to say that only a mother would have given such a sum for the work, but perhaps her object in the arrangement was to teach him not to neglect the occupation of husbandry, which in those days afforded a sure reward of rude comfort and domestic plenty. But from the time that he owned this periagua it may be doubted if he ever again took hold of the plow. His hand had closed firmly upon the tiller which for the next half century was to be to him a veritable sceptre.

From May 27, 1810, it may be considered that Cornelius Vanderbilt put away childish things and became a man, earning his own livelihood and able to take his own part in the affairs of the world. He was but 16, but he had no difficulty in obtaining passengers for his ferry boat, especially, it may be presumed, among the fairer portion of the Staten Islanders. For the young man was tall, vigorous, broad of shoulder, bright of eye, possessed of a complexion that any belle might envy, and having a very sweet and engaging smile, which all the cares of a very extraordinary and busy life never effaced from his countenance.

Not only did his periagua find constant occupation, but he purchased interests in other boats, and chartered more, so that when the war broke out in 1812 he was quite a thriving man, and even then a personage in his own peculiar line. Young Cornele, as everybody called him, was the first person thought of when anything very dangerous or very disagreeable had to be done. When the winds were high and the sight was blinded with driving sleet and snow, and the waves raged like angry wolves, if an important message had to be sent from the forts to the headquarters in the City, young Cornele was sent for. When the British fleet tried to force their way past Sandy Hook to lay New York in ashes, as the Admiral kindly promised, the forts on Sandy Hook beat them off. A fearful storm was raging, but it was absolutely necessary to notify the commanding officer in the City of the attempt and its repulse, and to obtain reinforcements and fresh supplies in case of a renewal. A messenger was sent for the only man who could take a boat through the raging waters to the Battery slip.

When Cornele Vanderbilt made his appearance, the staff officer asked anxiously if a boat could live in such a sea. "Yes," said Cornelius, laconically, but firmly, "if properly handled." "Will you take us to the Battery," was the next question. "I will," replied the young man, "but you will be underwater half the time." He landed them in safety at the stairs, but they were like drowned rats, and such had been the fury of the winds and waters and the incessant movements of the boat, that one of them declared he had not had time to draw one full breath.

JAY GOULD (MAY 27, 1836 – DECEMBER 2, 1892)

THE BURLINGTON HAWK EYE, IOWA, DECEMBER 3, 1892

*N*ew York, December 2 — The history of Jay Gould, from the barefooted boy who wandered over the rough hills of Delaware county to the railroad king whose wealth was estimated at $100,000,000, is one of the most remarkable among our self-made men.

His life for the last few months has been a constant battle against the inevitable, and all means that medical skill and the interest of friends and relatives could suggest were employed to prolong the financier's life. He was taken about in luxurious private cars to places where milder air and the absence of business excitement might be expected to work a recuperation of his energies.

Jay Gould was born in West Settlement, a backwoods village of Roxbury, Delaware county, New York, on May 27, 1836. He was the son of John B. Gould, a farmer, who was fairly well-to-do, and who had been a deputy sheriff in the famous anti-rent war in the early '20s. Young Gould was also a cousin of Alvord Gould, the inventor of the chain well pump, and was closely connected with the Mores, a prominent Scotch family, and others well known in the county. His mother died when he was an infant.

Mr Gould left home with 50 cents in his jacket and studied at Hobart academy, in a neighboring town. He earned an extra penny by keeping books for the village blacksmith, eventually enjoying a brief partnership in the business.

He was fond of mathematics, and on leaving school found employment in making surveys for a map of Ulster county at a salary of $20 per month. The correctness of the work attracted the attention of John Delafield, who applied to the legislature to authorize a map of the state to be made, in which Mr Gould would have a prominent part of the work. The work failed, owing to the death of the promoter, and Mr Gould, having gained $3,000 or $4,000 through his previous maps and surveys, wrote a *History of Delaware County*.

After an unsuccessful attempt to push the sale of a patent mouse trap which he had invented, Mr Gould entered into partnership with Zadock Pratt in the tannery business. In 1856, the patent was sold, and Gould came to New York with quite an addition to his fortune. He entered into business with Charles Leupp, leather merchant. In the panic of 1857, Leupp's capital was wrecked, but Gould managed to come through without severe loss.

Gould's father-in-law, Mr Daniel S. Miller, initiated the young financier into the railroad business and sold him a number of shares in the Rutland and Washington railroad at 10 cents on the dollar. Gould showed so much interest that he was soon elected president and general manager of the road, and finally consolidated it with the Rensselaer and Saratoga railroad. When the stock went up, Gould sold out at a handsome profit.

In the year of 1858, Jay Gould entered Wall Street as a broker. He established a small private office and made money fast. The following year, he entered the firm of Smith & Martin and became an expert in the handling of railroad securities. During the civil war, Erie railroad stock went down to bedrock and Gould bought it for a song. He allied himself with Daniel Drew and prevented Commodore Vanderbilt from cornering the Erie interest. Gould rapidly became the leading spirit of the Erie railroad company. In July 1867, Gould was made president of the road. He also purchased a controlling interest in the Tenth National Bank. Erie shareholders brought suit to restrain the directors from issuing any more stock. The complainants asked for the appointment of a receiver. The request was granted by the appointment of Jay Gould himself. With the consent of Judge George G. Barnard, Gould bought and cancelled 200,000 shares. A corner was engineered in Erie stock about this time and in one day its price rose from 40 to 60. A panic was averted by the action of the secretary of the treasury, who released enough money for the sub-treasury to relieve the strain. Erie immediately fell from 60 to 42, and it was thought Gould was ruined. But he was able to weather the storm. Continued efforts were made by Gould's opponents to oust him and his faction from Erie control, and he was deposed from the presidency and John A. Dix elected in his place. Gould still remained one of the directors.

No two estimates agree as to the amount of Mr Gould's fortune. The most conservative figures place it at about $75,000,000, while some people in Wall Street, who think they know something about his accumulations, figure that he must have amassed fully $150,000,000. His known holdings of securities are about as follows: 22,000,000 par value of Western Union, which at today's prices would fetch about

$18,700,000; $10,000,000 par value of Missouri Pacific, which is now worth in the market $5,500,000. He is supposed to hold in the neighborhood of $8,000,000 worth of Manhattan railway stock, worth $10,400,000. His holdings of all these stocks have been larger, but he sold them to either invest the money in new issues of bonds of the Missouri Pacific and Manhattan companies or to finance those companies until bonds could be issued.

Excellent information is that he holds about one-third of the bonds issued on the Missouri Pacific system, which would be about $30,000,000. His estate holds over $12,000,000 of Wabash railway stock, which shows a loss of between $4,000,000 and $5,000,000. As long ago as 1884, Mr Gould was known to hold about $3,000,000 of first-class railway mortgage bonds upon roads other than those controlled or managed by him. Besides these, he had large investments in a great number of properties concerning which the general public knows little or nothing. His holdings of Union Pacific and Kansas Pacific bonds, which have never been stated, must be large, but it is not believed that he owned of late years much, if any, Union Pacific stock.

From the foregoing figures it is easy to figure up in the neighborhood of $75,000,000. Of late years, his fortune has increased rapidly, owing to his enormous income from his holdings of Western Union and Manhattan stock, to say nothing of his investments in bonds. His income from these three sources alone cannot have fallen under $3,000,000 a year, and has probably exceeded that amount.

Mr Gould is said to have given to his sons, George, Edwin and Howard, in the neighborhood of $5,000,000, mostly in bonds. In addition, George Gould holds $40,000,000 of stock in the Pacific Mall, Missouri Pacific and some other valuable stock. It was said over a year ago when Mr Gould was very ill that he would leave no will, but that he had already disposed of his great wealth. Each child and relative who had any demand on him had received, it was said, a fair share of the estate and had given receipt for it, Mr Gould simply holding it in trust until his death. This course was taken to avoid legal squabbling after his death.

Mr Gould's children are said to know just how much each will receive, and every one of them is satisfied with the way Mr Gould distributed his estate. George Gould was designated the guardian of his two minor brothers and sister. Of the other children, Edwin, who was married to Miss Sarah Shrady only a month ago, is 27, Howard is 24, and Helen, who was her father's secretary and his constant companion since Mrs Gould's death four years ago, is 23. The other children are aged 19 and 17 respectively. Mr Gould was the grandfather of three children, all girls, the daughters of his son George.

Mrs George Gould was Miss Edith Kingdon, for three or four years an actress in Daly's company. Edwin is the only other married child. Miss Helen has never encouraged the many attentions showered upon her by the swains of New York society men. She is not considered a marrying girl.

When he was operating on a large scale, Mr Gould's first step in a deal was to get the outsiders on the wrong track. He made people believe he was doing exactly the opposite of what in fact he was. If he desired to unload stocks, he would talk them up and have the brokers who were known to do business for him buy them. But he would have other brokers sell three times as many stocks as were bought for him. If he desired to acquire stocks, he would pursue the reverse tactics. His plan was to buy on a declining scale and sell on an advancing scale. It reads like a simple transaction, but the thing is to keep the market going down or up as may be to the advantage of the speculator, and here was where Mr Gould showed his consummate art.

Mr Gould did not always come out of a deal with a profit. He has been "cornered" and made to pay dearly for the stocks he needed to make his deliveries, and again he has been left with a large accumulation of stocks on his hands that he had to sell for much less than he bought them. But, of course, his speculative account shows a vast balance in his favor.

No one in Wall Street will ever forget the terrible May panic of 1884. House after house was wrecked and fortune after fortune was lost. It was nearly as bad as the famous "'73 panic". Some of the greatest financiers came near being dragged down, Jay Gould among the number. He was loaded with long stocks and was a borrower of money to the extent of millions. When the enormous decline in values occurred, he was called upon for additional collateral on the loans he had obtained. He was obliged to comply with the demands or else pay off his loans. He had no more stocks or bonds to pledge and he could not borrow from the banks, trust companies or other lenders of money. The idea of an assignment was considered by Mr Gould. Had it been carried out, disaster would have extended from one end of the country to the other. Mr Gould was by no means insolvent at the time. The question was whether an assignment would not keep his assets together in case of further depreciation in the stock market. There was no doubt that sooner or later there would be a recovery that would place him where he was before the panic.

The New York Sun, December 3, 1892

JAY GOULD WAS A SHORT, spare man, with piercing black eyes and a sallow face, the lower part of which was hidden behind a full black beard. Those who knew him best said that it was through his eyes that the man revealed himself. They were a remarkable pair - searching, firm, cold and all but incapable of changing in any way that might betray his feelings. He seldom lost his temper or was excited. His methods, if his friends analyze them correctly, led him to discern public movements before his rivals did, and to follow rather than to lead them. Thus he got the great influence of natural forces to add to his power and weight in many important railway speculations. In others, he created conditions to suit his speculative intentions, and there were no means he would hesitate to adopt in order to succeed.

The New York Herald, December 3, 1892

MR GOULD WAS NEVER a robust person. He was below medium height, thin, nervous and reticent, his hair, eyes and head were jet black. He was fastidious in dress, and never approached the gaucheries that marked and marred his lieutenant, James Fisk. Gould was all brain and nerve. Fisk all drive and muscle. Although quiet, imperturbable and indisposed to confidences, Mr Gould's expression was by no means unpleasant. On the contrary, he was, in a sense, companionable. He was extremely fond of home comforts and never permitted business to interfere with his 2 o'clock dinner or his afternoon drive. In manner, he was kind and gentle. Never averse to give an opinion, unless it interfered with a plan, he was careful not to obtrude one.

The St James's Gazette, London, December 3, 1892

THE MOST TYPICAL MARAUDER of the age is dead. In his reckless contempt for honor, justice, mercy or morality, he transcends the giant speculators of the world. He leaves a hundred millions of dollars accumulated by gambling, swindling and fraud. We don't like to speak ill of the dead, but there is no other way to describe Gould and the methods by which he acquired his enormous fortune.

The Daily News, London, December 3, 1892

IT WAS MR GOULD'S AMBITION to be the richest man in the world, but be died disappointed. The Vanderbilts, Astors and Rockefellers beat him. Yet all honor to the greatest money-maker of any age or clime. He was less a man than a machine for churning wealth. Napoleon's combinations were never vaster, and there were many points of resemblance between the two men. It will be impossible to explain one phase of civilization without a frequent mention of Mr Gould's name; therefore, he is sure of a place in history.

The Times, London, December 3, 1892

MR GOULD'S DEATH MEANS the removal of a disturbing influence of vast and incalculable force. The man and the position he held were products of American life. Such a career could hardly have been possible elsewhere than in America. Money is raised in America to a rank higher than it can usefully occupy, owing to the absence of class distinctions. He was one of the most remarkable Americans of the last half of the century. No other man unaided by family influence, friends or luck has written himself so deeply into the financial history of the republic. No other man exercised such a baneful influence on the moral character of the community. Yet the side which he kept hidden from the world was in many ways in striking contrast. He was never accused of ostentation, and all acquainted with his home life have but one opinion to express, and that is a very kindly one.

The Standard, December 3, 1892

NO HONEST BIOGRAPHER can adhere to the maxim "Deal charitably with the dead" when this wrecker of industries and impoverisher of men comes up for Judgment. It is impossible to point to a single enterprise that he benefited, or to a solitary act of self-sacrifice on his part. It would be affectation to pretend that the world is made poorer by his departure.

Werner Siemens (December 13, 1816 – December 6, 1892)

The Scotsman, December 7, 1892

A telegram from Berlin, through Reuter's Agency, announces the death there last evening of Werner von Siemens, the eldest of a family of engineers of worldwide renown. The representative of the family in this country was the late Sir William Siemens, whoso name is so prominently associated with the application of electricity, with the extension of the telegraph in almost all parts of the world, and with important discoveries which almost revolutionised the process of the production of steel.

Werner Siemens was the eldest of the family, and was born in Lenthe, in Hanover, in December 1816. His scientific tastes were early made manifest. He was associated with his brother in an invention connected with electroplating, which made the fortune of the late Sir William. The latter sold the invention to a firm in Birmingham, and in a letter which he subsequently wrote to friends in Germany he said he had come to England a poor lad, and might leave it a comparative Croesus.

Werner Siemens subsequently improved on this invention - in its application to gold as well as to silver plating. Sir William Siemens made England his home. Werner stuck to Germany. In 1834, he entered the Prussian artillery, and 10 years later we find him in charge of the artillery depot of Berlin.

When he entered German society as a civil engineer, he devoted himself to the study of applied science, chiefly in the department of electricity. The telegraph system of Prussia was developed under his supervision, and it was while he was engaged in this work that he discovered the insulating property of gutta percha - a discovery which has played an important part in the extension of the telegraph, particularly by submarine and underground cables. He constructed one of the first great lines of telegraph on the Continent - that between Berlin and Frankfurt in 1847.

Six of the Atlantic cables, as well as submarine cables in other parts of the world, were laid by Messrs Siemens Brothers (Limited), to the formation of which company Werner von Siemens chiefly contributed. As the head of the firm of Siemens & Halske of Berlin, established in 1847, he was the leader of his profession in Germany, and he was also well known by reputation to British scientists. He was an honorary member of the British Institute of Electrical Engineers, as also of the British Association. Of the Berlin firm of Siemens & Halske there were founded branches in London, St Petersburg and Vienna.

In the *Life of Sir William Siemens*, published a few years ago by Mr John Murray, the letters of the subject of that work bore ample testimony to the commanding ability and genius of his elder brother, and fully described how he invented the dynamo-electric machine which we associate with his name, the pneumatic tube system, and other things that are in daily use in the community. Werner assisted Sir William also in the development of his conception of the electrical transmission of power, and in the application of electricity to traction purposes. In 1874, he was elected a member of the Berlin Academy, and numerous scientific papers from his pen are published in the transactions of that body. In 1886, he presented to Berlin the sum of 500,000 marks (£25,000) for the purpose of founding an Imperial Institute of Technical Education. He was in 1888 ennobled by the German Emperor. He was the recipient of honours also at the hands of several German Universities.

The death of Dr Von Siemens was not unexpected. Several days ago, he was laid aside by an attack of influenza, and on Monday it was intimated that this was complicated by inflammation of the lungs.

WERNER SIEMENS (DECEMBER 13, 1816 – DECEMBER 6, 1892)

THE SCOTSMAN, DECEMBER 7, 1892

A telegram from Berlin, through Reuter's Agency, announces the death there last evening of Werner von Siemens, the eldest of a family of engineers of world-wide renown. The representative of the family in this country was the late Sir William Siemens, whoso name is so prominently associated with the application of electricity, with the extension of the telegraph in almost all parts of the world, and with important discoveries which almost revolutionised the process of the production of steel.

Werner Siemens was the eldest of the family, and was born in Lenthe, in Hanover, in December 1816. His scientific tastes were early made manifest. He was associated with his brother in an invention connected with electroplating, which made the fortune of the late Sir William. The latter sold the invention to a firm in Birmingham, and in a letter which he subsequently wrote to friends in Germany he said he had come to England a poor lad, and might leave it a comparative Croesus.

Werner Siemens subsequently improved on this invention - in its application to gold as well as to silver plating. Sir

William Siemens made England his home. Werner stuck to Germany. In 1834, he entered the Prussian artillery, and 10 years later we find him in charge of the artillery depot of Berlin.

When he entered German society as a civil engineer, he devoted himself to the study of applied science, chiefly in the department of electricity. The telegraph system of Prussia was developed under his supervision, and it was while he was engaged in this work that he discovered the insulating property of gutta percha - a discovery which has played an important part in the extension of the telegraph, particularly by submarine and underground cables. He constructed one of the first great lines of telegraph on the Continent - that between Berlin and Frankfurt in 1847.

Six of the Atlantic cables, as well as submarine cables in other parts of the world, were laid by Messrs Siemens Brothers (Limited), to the formation of which company Werner von Siemens chiefly contributed. As the head of the firm of Siemens & Halske of Berlin, established in 1847, he was the leader of his profession in Germany, and he was also well known by reputation to British scientists. He was an honorary member of the British Institute of Electrical Engineers, as also of the British Association. Of the Berlin firm of Siemens & Halske there were founded branches in London, St Petersburg and Vienna.

In the *Life of Sir William Siemens*, published a few years ago by Mr John Murray, the letters of the subject of that work bore ample testimony to the commanding ability and genius of his elder brother, and fully described how he invented the dynamo-electric machine which we associate with his name, the pneumatic tube system, and other things that are in daily use in the community. Werner assisted Sir William also in the development of his conception of the electrical transmission of power, and in the application of electricity to traction purposes. In 1874, he was elected a member of the Berlin Academy, and numerous scientific papers from his pen are published in the transactions of that body. In 1886, he presented to Berlin the sum of 500,000 marks (£25,000) for the purpose of founding an Imperial Institute of Technical Education. He was in 1888 ennobled by the German Emperor. He was the recipient of honours also at the hands of several German Universities.

The death of Dr Von Siemens was not unexpected. Several days ago, he was laid aside by an attack of influenza, and on Monday it was intimated that this was complicated by inflammation of the lungs.

6

LELAND STANFORD (MARCH 9, 1824 - JUNE 21, 1893)

THE PHILADELPHIA TIMES, JUNE 22, 1893

*U*nited States Senator Leland Stanford died last night at his residence in Palo Alto. Senator Stanford was in the best of spirits yesterday. He took a drive around his stock farm and seemed as well as ever. He went to bed soon after 10 o'clock, and at about midnight his valet going into the Senator's bedroom discovered that he was dead. It has been long evident that Senator Stanford's death was a question of but a short time. His symptoms were apoplectic, and his weight was increasing alarmingly.

Leland Stanford was born in Watervliet, Albany County, New York, March 9, 1824. Brought up on a farm, at 20 he studied law and was admitted in 1849. He immediately removed to Wisconsin and practiced at Port Washington. In 1852, having lost his law library and other property by fire, he started across the plains to join his three brothers, who had preceded him to California. They went into placer mining at Michigan Bluff. Mr Stanford was successful, and in 1859 he removed to San Francisco and entered into mercantile pursuits on an extensive scale. He made money and laid the foundation for an enormous fortune, which has been estimated as high as $75,000,000.

He soon acquired great local reputation and influence, and in 1860 he was sent as a delegate to the Chicago Convention, which nominated Abraham Lincoln for the Presidency. This position gave popular satisfaction, and in 1861 he was nominated for the Governorship of the state, and was elected, holding the position during the early years of the war, where he greatly influenced the popular feeling in regard to the question of slavery, and had much to do in bringing California into the Union column.

He had from the first been an aggressive and ardent exponent of the needs of the Pacific coast for railroad communication with the East, and in 1861, when the Central Pacific Railroad was organized, he was made its president. For eight years, he labored unremittingly, and on May 10, 1869, he drove the last spike at Promontory Point, Utah. Some idea of his force and energy may be gathered from the fact that in 293 days he built 520 miles of the road, and the completion of the great undertaking within so few years from its inception was considered as a remarkable piece of business enterprise.

He first took his seat as Senator on March 4, 1886. He early acquired respect and influence in national politics on the Republican side, and on the completion of his term in 1872 was again elected. His fealty was always to his State and her interests, but he never allowed his judgment to be clouded by picayune considerations, and his statesmanship was broad and catholic.

For years, he was famous for his generosity and princely gifts to worthy individuals and institutions, but his crowning philanthropy was the gift of $20,000,000 to the State of California to endow a university in memory of his only son,

Leland Stanford Jr, who died some years ago when only a mere boy. The cornerstone was laid on May 14, 1887. Since then, Mr Stanford has been energetic in obtaining the best equipment and instructors for his favorite project, which is situated on his immense estate at Palo Alto.

Not only is the university designed to give the ordinary educational advantages, but is as well a training school for those who must depend on their manual training for their subsistence. It is the greatest result of the kind ever accomplished by the liberality of one man, and will be a lasting tribute to his memory and that of his son, as well as of constant use and benefit to the whole Pacific coast.

As a breeder of blood horses, he has, by his enterprise and liberality, given California a place equal if not superior to that of Kentucky. The fame of his Palo Alto stable is not dimmed by the greatest achievements of the renowned Bluegrass region. In fact, no other breeder in the world has ever obtained such a turf record for an individual stable. At one time, his horses, all trotters, won the record for all ages, most of which they still hold. This result is due mostly to the Governor's original theory of breeding trotting stock, to which, despite his many other vast interests, be paid close attention.

His chief characteristics were his broad humanity and his intense energy. His gifts varied from $1 to $20,000,000, but they were always given carefully and, though generous to an excess, his charity was guarded by good sense and he was never carried away by the mere egotism of giving into the foolish expenditure of even the smallest sums when they were likely to be misapplied.

The last few years of his life were saddened by the loss of his only child, whose death softened the rugged places in his character and gave him a tenderness and sweetness with all suffering and misfortune which endeared him to all who met him to a wonderful degree. It is no empty eulogy, but a statement of simple fact to say that no man has had a larger influence on the general history of California and no man will be more missed on the Pacific coast than the venerable Senator who passed away early this morning.

7

ALFRED NOBEL (OCTOBER 21, 1833 – DECEMBER 10, 1896)

THE DAILY TELEGRAPH, LONDON, DECEMBER 11, 1896

We regret to announce the death of Mr Alfred Nobel, which took place yesterday at his villa in Sanremo. Were we to say that the scientific discoverer and chemist who has just expired was, as *The Quarterly Review* dubbed him in April 1883 "the greatest inventor and maker of blasting explosives in the world", we should be preparing a strange surprise for those who, ignorant of his calling, saw in the modest and retiring son of a Swedish-Finn father and a Scottish mother nothing to connect him with the dynamitards of the Clan-na-Gael or the pétroleuses of the Paris commune.

In truth, Mr Alfred Nobel had no more to do with the Fenian conspirators of New York and Chicago, or with the human fiends, male and female, who, calling themselves Anarchists, dabble in scattering fire and destruction among the homes of peaceful, law-abiding citizens all over the world, than the physician who includes "nux vomica" among the ingredients of a tonic which he prescribes for his patients has with the preparation of deadly poisons.

The great step in advance that science owes to Mr Nobel

was well described by him in a paper, "On Modern Blasting Agents", which he read before the Society of Arts in May 1875, wherein he put the difficulties of disestablishing gunpowder as the king of explosives in the clearest light. "It is not sufficient," he said, "that a substance is explosive to render it useful for practical purposes. A great many questions have first to be considered; whether, for instance, it compares favourably with competing substances already in use; whether the same power can be lodged in the same bulk, and what the cost and risk of its manufacture is; whether its carriage and use are not too dangerous for practical employment; whether its chemical stability can withstand influence by any or all climates; how, again, it is affected by water; and finally, what effect its gases and fumes when exploded produce on the health of miners. This explains why, with more powerful explosives at command, it is so hard to supersede gunpowder. That old mixture, five and a half centuries old, possesses wonderful elasticity, permitting its adaptation to purposes of the most varied nature. Thus, in a mine, it blasts without propelling; in a gun, it propels without blasting; in a shell, it served both purposes combined; in a fuse and in fireworks, it burns slowly without exploding. Its pressure, exercised in these numerous operations, varies between one ounce to the square inch in a fuse and 85,000lb to the square inch in a shell. But, like a servant-of-all-work, it lacks perfection in each department, and modern science, armed with better tools, is gradually encroaching on gunpowder's old domain."

It would be far beyond the limits of space at our command to rehearse even the names of the chemists of various nations to whose cumulative labour we owe that king or giant of modern explosives, blasting gelatine. Suffice it for our present purpose to say that Alfred Nobel must, for all future time, hold a very prominent position. France, peculiarly rich, not only politically but also scientifically, in explosive minds, began by giving us Théophile Pelouze, of Paris, who, aided by his assistant and co-labourer Ascanio Sobrero, an Italian, first discovered that sweet, viscous liquid called nitro-glycerine. These two giants among experimental chemists were soon succeeded and improved upon by Frederich Schönbein, and by Baron Lenk, of Austria, who simultaneously discovered gun-cotton, and communicated the contagion of their discovery to Sir Frederick Abel, long and widely famed as the chemical expert of our War Department, and, perhaps, the last scientific believer in the wonderful shattering forces and adaptability of military uses of discs of wet pyrosyline and gun-cotton.

We are now approaching the time when Mr Alfred Nobel, hitherto unknown as a Swedish engineer and chemist, was to make civil and military engineers familiar with the most tremendous blasting agent that the world has thus far known. At the moment when Alfred Nobel was coming upon the scene, gun-cotton, which Professor Sir F Abel had theretofore believed was explosible only by detonation, and never by spontaneous ignition, was, to use the language of the Turf, "scratched" in the race of explosives for which it was entered by the fearful catastrophe which took place at the Stowmarket gun-cotton factory in 1871. The catastrophe in question was caused by a box of gun-cotton, which accidently took fire. The flames soon extended to a large pile of boxes, full also of gun-cotton. The two Messrs Prentice (William and Edward), managers of the factory, drew a box out of the pile to prevent the conflagration from spreading, and, thinking that gun-cotton would only explode from detonation, threw the box, heated as it was by the contiguous flames, to the ground, from a height of some feet. It struck the ground violently and exploded, killing them both. A few minutes later, the pile of of gun-cotton boxes also exploded spontaneously, killing 22 other persons, and almost shattering the little Suffolk town of Stowmarket. The tragic accident clearly showed that the chemical stability of gun-cotton, or, in other words, its dangerous liability to spontaneous decomposition from heat, excluded it from further competition with explosives of the nitroglyc-erine family.

About that time, Mr Nobel was commencing his experi-ments with nitroglycerine as a blasting agent, and also for employment in guns and cannon. In 1864, the now famous Swedish engineer, who died yesterday, began to deal with "the sweet-tasting, oily, colourless liquid" which Sobrero, acting under Pelouze, had brought to perfection in Paris in 1847. The first act of ingratitude performed by the new agent was to blow up Mr Nobel's factory near Stockholm in 1868, killing nearly 20 persons. In December of the previous winter, while the frost was intense, the Mayor of Newcastle-on-Tyne undertook to bury some frozen nitroglycerine in the town moor, because no one knew what to do with the dangerous compound. Struck by a spade, one of the frozen morsels exploded, killing seven persons. Many similar acci-dents in North, South and Central America showed that liquid or frozen nitroglycerine was liable, under certain conditions, to spontaneous decomposition and, therefore, Mr Nobel resolved to discontinue its manufacture, and to hunt for an absorbent capable of drinking up enough of the explosive to be available for blasting purposes, and of turning it into a comparatively harmless solid.

Such an absorbent he discovered in a siliceous earth, called in German "kieselguhr", with a low specific gravity, and composed of the remains of infusorial insects. It abounds in many parts of the Continent, and especially in Hanover, and, according to Mr Henry Drinker, a member of the American Institute of Mining Engineers, and author of that able work *Tunnelling, Explosive Compounds, and Rock Drills*, published in New York in 1878, it is also found in the state of New Jersey. Finally, we hear from Mr George McRoberts, who is head of of the Nobel Blasting Factories in Ayrshire and Stirlingshire, that "kieselguhr" also abounds in Aberdeenshire.

The first great debt that consumers of blasting agents - and their name is legion - all over the world owe to Mr Alfred Nobel is that, by importing "kieselguhr" into the manufacture of nitroglycerine, he invented what is familiarly known to us in Europe as "dynamite", and in the United States as "giant powder". For dynamite, as prepared by his process, Mr Nobel took out, in 1867 and 1868, patents all over the world, and until his discovery later on of blasting gelatine, about which we shall presently have a few words to say, dynamite was recognised and universally used as the champion blasting agent of civilisation. It will be understood that, mixed with a porous earth, created in the laboratory of Nature, and first utilised for this purpose by Alfred Nobel, nitroglycerine takes the form of dynamite, becomes capable of safe transportation, and is easily manageable. To explode it in small quantities, heat and strong percussion are needed.

"It is therefore," according to the instructions sent forth by its inventor, "prepared for blasting by the insertion of a cap or exploder of fulminating powder, which may be fired either by a fuse or by the electric current." In point of fact, general opinion had decided in Europe, Asia, Africa, Australia and America, where great tearing, rending, strength and safety of transport are needed, that Alfred Nobel's "No1 Dynamite" was the best blasting agent known to commerce.

Had Alfred Nobel died in 1881, the discovery and utilisation of this marvellous explosive would alone have sufficed to give such immortality to his name as human beings are capable of conferring. It was reserved for his honour to discover in the last 15 years of his indefatigably active, industrious and useful life another blasting agent, compared to which dynamite is "what moonlight is to sunlight, or as water is to wine". Seeing that his dynamite is, in his own words, "but a weakened solidification of liquid nitroglycerine", Alfred Nobel's ingenious mind sought for another ingredient, which, taking the place of that weakening element, "kieselguhr", or porous, siliceous earth, might, in combination with the explosive liquid, add to the strength of the compound. Such an ingredient as found ready to hand in nitro-cotton, itself an explosive, blended with thoroughly purified nitroglycerine. The blend, or combination, is in the proportion of seven parts of nitro-cotton in every hundred parts of nitroglycerine.

The new discovery had an excellent "send off" when, in the March of 1883, Professor (now Sir Frederick) Abel read a paper before the Glasgow Science Lectures Association enthusiastically approving of blasting gelatine as the cheapest, strongest and safest blasting agent yet known to chemistry. We believe that since then, Sir F Abel, aided by Dr August Dupré, chemical adviser of the Home Office, and by Colonel Vivian Dering Majendie, RA, Chief Inspector of Explosives, have slightly modified the blasting gelatine prepared by Mr Nobel's accomplished Scotch coadjutor Mr - or, as we believe he is sometimes called, "Professor" - George McRoberts, who is in command of the Nobel factory at

Ardeer, near Irvine, Ayrshire. The fact, however, remains that as inventor or originator first of dynamite, then of blasting galatine, Mr Nobel had no compeer or rival to dispute his claims to be regarded as King of Explosives all over the world.

Much might be added to illustrate the life history and character of the remarkable man who died yesterday, and who, during his visits to this country, held a kind of court and kept open house at the Westminster Palace Hotel. With the able assistance of Dr Thorne, his chief agent in this country who was always to be found at the Nobel office in Gracechurch Street, Mr Nobel surrounded himself with clever men in every walk of life, and was never satisfied unless they took two or three meals at his table every day.

To tell the truth, the vast wealth of the three Nobel brothers, Ludwig (who died in 1888), Robert and Alfred, justified each and all of them in the indulgence of the most profuse expenditure. In addition to the factories of explosive "bossed" by Alfred Nobel in Scotland and Sweden, the other two brothers developed and turned to most profitable account the great petroleum resources and grounds lying near Baku, a Russian town on the Caspian. The 34 million gallons of rock oil yielded by Baku in 1875 had grown to 200 million in 1882, and the exportation is now enormous and always increasing. In quality, it does not equal the petroleum sent forth from the United States by the Standard Oil Company, which has within a few years created the prodigious wealth of the Rockefellers and their partners. The American producers and exporters of petroleum have, however, attained their enormous fortunes by skilful management of Nature's resources.

Apart from Baku, the Nobel brothers belong to that mighty and world-mastering class described by the gifted author of *Philip van Artevelde*, when he wrote, "The world knows nothing of its greatest men." In practical and sagacious discoveries, and in perfecting and maturing those discoveries, the world has produced few equals to the three Nobel brothers; and of them the greatest was Alfred.

The Scotsman, December 11, 1896

SANREMO, DECEMBER 10 - Mr Alfred Nobel, the Swedish engineer and chemist, died last night at his villa here. The deceased was the first to recognise the value of nitroglycerine, which he introduced as a blasting agent for industrial purposes.

The manufacture of dynamite is an important industry in the west of Scotland, and in the creation and fostering of that industry Mr Nobel played an important part. In cooperation with a number of Glasgow gentlemen, he formed the British Dynamite Company, which acquired his patent, and erected works for the manufacture of the new explosive at Ardeer, near Stevenston, in Ayrshire. These works were at a later date taken over by Nobel's Explosives Company (Limited), whose head offices are in Glasgow.

Some 15 years ago, Mr Nobel invented an improvement on dynamite, known as blasting gelatine, the compound now mostly used instead of dynamite. He was also the inventor of balastite, the new smokeless powder, of which cordite was alleged to be an imitation. Nobel's Explosives Company, who acquired the ballistite patent, sued the Government a year or two ago for infringement, but they were not successful in establishing their case.

The Ardeer works, where balistite and other explosives are manufactured, employ about 1,200 hands. The

Company has also manufactories at Westquarter and Redding Moor, near Polmont and at Perranporth, Cornwall.

Mr Nobel resided for many years in Paris, and carried on his experiments there. The French Government, however, took exception because he sold his patents to a foreign Government, and he was compelled to leave France. He transferred his headquarters then to Sanremo in the north of Italy, and there erected a large laboratory. In the course of his business, he paid several visits to Glasgow, but a number of years have passed since he was last in the city.

8

BARNEY BARNATO (FEBRUARY 21, 1851 - JUNE 14, 1897)

THE BURLINGTON EVENING GAZETTE, IOWA, JUNE 15, 1897

*L*ondon, June 15. Barney Barnato, the famous Kaffir King, who has made millions of dollars in the last few years by developing the celebrated gold and diamond mines in South Africa, committed suicide by jumping from the steamer Scot in the Atlantic ocean while en route to his home in England. He left Cape Town on June 2 and would have reached home today.

He had been ill for some time, and it is supposed the act was committed while in a fit of depression. No other reason is given for his strange act.

Barney Barnato was a mystery as well as a marvel. This king of kaffirs, this real Monte Cristo, appeared suddenly from nowhere, astonished the world with his wealth, threw the stock market into a raging fever, was fêted by the distinguished personages whom he enriched, and, in turn, was execrated by the thousands who suffered in the reaction.

The most contradictory and fantastic tales were told of him. His early life was shrouded in mystery and he dazed the world like a comet. No two accounts of his origin agree. His name seems to have been Bernard Isaac Barnato. One story gave his surname as Isaacs. Barney was said to be the diminutive of Barnabas, but Barnato was also quoted as explaining it came from Barnet. In London, it is commonly believed that he was the son of a poor Hebrew schoolmaster in the East End; that he was once a cab driver, and after that a peddler of second-hand clothing in Petticoat Lane, his specialty being waistcoats.

It is said he was subsequently a billiard marker, and that two years after the discovery of diamonds in South Africa, he emigrated to the Transvaal with his his brother, who had been a juggler in cheap circuses and "penny gaffs". This was in 1872, if Whitechapel chronology does not err. Barney was then 20 years old. Barnato and his brother had exhausted their capital in passage money, but they made $100 on the trip to Africa by entertaining their shipmates and passing around the hat. Arrived in the new country, Barney and his brother struck out for the diamond fields, where they began a new life. The rest is mere money-making.

A very different story is told by a London financial journal. This is a summary of the revised version: "Mr Barnet I. Barnato was born in London on July 5, 1852. He is the third son of Mr Isaac Barnato, of Devonshire Terrace, Hyde Park, and on his mother's side is connected with the late Sir George Jessel, who was well known as a lawyer, a judge and master of the rolls. Mr Barnato passed his boyhood in London, and was educated at private scholastic establishments by private tutors. At an early age, he entered the commercial world, but he threw off the harness of humdrum duties to search fresh fields and pastures new in South Africa.

"In 1873, on his twenty-first birthday, he sailed from London on the ship Anglian. His first African ventures were successful; at the end of three years, he owned diamond mines in the neighborhood of Kimberley, and in 1881 he sold these mines to a company for $575,000." And so on.

What is definitely known is that three or four years ago, Barney Barnato returned to London the possessor of "untold gold". The reports of his wealth varied with the imagination of the reporters. But it did not take long to discover that in South Africa, Barnato had been a power. He was the shrewdest of speculators in that distant region. When diamond mining was being overdone, when mines were multiplying and competition was bringing prices down with a run, timid men lost heart and abandoned or cheaply sold their claims.

Barney Barnato had the foresight to acquire what the weak ones were glad to be rid of, and when Cecil Rhodes appeared with his Napoleonic plan for amalgamating all diamond mining interests of South Africa in order to control the output and the price, it was discovered that the industrious Barney owned a large tract of "claims" in the best part of Kimberley.

Cecil Rhodes' mighty plans and great successes in the colonization and development of South Africa began to assume imperial dimensions. Another continent might come under the rule of the Anglo-Saxon. The pride and the pockets of England were touched. Men and money poured into the cape, and from the cape northward to Mashona-land, at the beckoning of the "Caesar of the south". Mr Rhodes, visiting England, was welcomed like a conquering hero. Africa the golden was the theme of public discussion and private conference everywhere. A new empire was rising in the hitherto dark to strike, and strike home. He reached England on the crest of the South African tidal wave. He was the first millionaire from that distant realm. He owned some 30 mines - some 2,500 "claims". The properties in which he was interested produced a revenue of $25,000,000 a year. They were paying 24 per cent interest on their capital of $20,000,000. They promised to pay something like 40 per cent in the near future.

London passed from excitement into a fever of greed. Everybody with money to invest fell over his neighbor in haste to reach the brokers and gamble in the shares of the Barnato companies. For many days, the streets around the Stock Exchange were packed with eager speculators. Prices rose with every tick of the watch; fortune was piled on fortune; hundreds, thousands of men found themselves suddenly rich, and they lost their heads. There was a money madness in the air, and the praises of Barnato were loud on the lips of the multitude.

Then came the inevitable reaction. The raging fever had spent itself; the speculation had been overdone; the men who had lost their heads now lost their fortunes; prices tumbled about their ears, and "the street" was strewn with wreckage. Losing speculators forgot their own rashness and cursed Barnato. When the King of the Kaffirs proposed to spend $5,000,000 to bull the market, the defeated gamblers accused him of stock jobbing.

Barnato started a bank with a capital of $12,500,000, and its stock became worth $45,000,000. He made a move to get into the social swim. He leased Spencer House, in St James's Place, London, the town residence of the Red Earl, who in William Gladstone's fourth ministry was first lord of the admiralty, and in his third ministry lord lieutenant of Ireland. Spencer House is too costly a place for the earl to use for himself, so he lets it whenever he can find a wealthy tenant. A recent tenant was Mrs Marshall Roberts, the hospitable American lady who is now Mrs Ralph Vivian, and who has been known to pay $1,000 a week for the privilege of living during the fashionable season in the palace of the Spencers. Then Barnato began to build a magnificent mansion of his own in no less a thoroughfare than Park Lane.

Mr Barnato was married. Mrs Barnato is a handsome and agreeable woman, and formed, as they say, a fitting chatelaine for the great mansion. The Barnatos had three children - a daughter and two sons. The daughter, Leah, is the eldest child; she is about seven or eight years of age. The baby boy is named Ladas Rosebery Barnato. It is perhaps a curious kind of taste to name a child for a horse and its owner, even when the horse is a Derby winner and its owner an ex-prime minister. But one is to argue from this that the king of diamonds was an ardent sporting man. He showed no greater interest in the turf than the average Englishman who has a lot ot money to spare.

Barnato was a genial-natured man. His tastes and habits were those of the newly rich, though he did not break into parliament or take to yachting. At his office in London, he was as inaccessible as the Emperor of China. At the West End townhouse, he was at home to all comers. To all his friends he was "Barney". His favorite, and, indeed, only reception hour was the hour of breakfast. That meal he took with his wife and a thoroughbred bulldog.

A great man must have at least one eccentricity. Barney Barnato's was his socks, which were of white silk.

The wicked have no rest, nor the new rich any repose. Even at his breakfast table, Barnato was besieged. To him at that hour came all the cranks, and beggars, and flatterers, and wild-eyed projectors. He saw them all. An English reporter who was admitted to this levee found himself one of an incongruous crew. One man had come with well nigh a continent of land to sell - it only needed developing. There was a woman with a choice bit of old lace. Several gentlemen who had written highly meritorious plays were present to represent that they needed only a little capital to enrich the dramatic firmament. Some "pals" from the city had dropped in to ask how the new Aladdin was after the night's banquet. Some old professional friends of the circus days had a warm corner. And there were others. To one and all of these, Barney talked in turn, managing the while to advise his wife, play with his dog, counsel his son and admire his pretty daughter.

The swift dismissal of business, great or small, was one of Barney Barnato's strong points. "Don't be serious," he said to the English reporter. "I'm never serious out of business. Life is too short to be serious, and don't let that artist sketch my white socks."

Questioned as to his methods of business, and how he managed his multifarious affairs, he said: "I have got them all in my head or at my fingers' ends. I trust absolutely to memory, end never make any notes."

Barney Barnato had dramatic instincts and they helped him throughout his be-diamonded career. He seized the dramatic moment when he stood for election as candidate for the Cape Colony parliament, and was triumphantly elected as South Africa's millionaire, and her "greatest captain of industry". He seized the dramatic moment when he came to London, and took advantage of the tide of imperial sentiment which followed Cecil Rhodes. Losers may sneer because his friend, the speculative lord mayor, made him a "lieutenant of the city of London". and so gave him the right to wear a scarlet uniform, but that sinecure appointment is not droller than many others which are chronicled in various parts of the world.

In appearance, Mr Barnato was a typical modern

Englishman - one of the kind that is often seen on the stage and sometimes in caricatures. A little above medium height, he was rather heavily built, with an oval face and brown hair, which he wore parted in the middle and plastered right tightly to his head. His sandy mustache was cut short and twisted so tight at the ends that it had the appearance of being waxed. Near-sighted, he had acquired the habit of squinting, and though a pair of eyeglasses rendered his vision good, the muscles around his eyes were usually so contracted as to form a mass of wrinkles.

He liked to play billiards, and his favorite stake was threepence; he liked to play cards, but never for money; he enjoyed a good story and could tell one well himself. He enjoyed his home, but, as he said, did not see half enough of it. Such, in a way, was "Barney" Barnato, the man whose name attached to any company was sure to send its stock skyward until the par value had been tripled and quadrupled.

Two hundred years ago, John Law sent one ship to New Orleans and brought back an odd collection of American products. On the strength of that and his name, the Mississippi company was formed, and stock to the face value of millions of dollars was sold far above par. The Mississippi company went to smash and John Law died in poverty in Venice. Mr Barnato's companies have not gone to smash, and there was little chance of his dying in poverty, for English financial papers place the value of his estate at $100,000,000. It is an estimated value, however, and aside from some landed estates may consist of almost anything.

It is beyond doubt largely composed of stocks in the companies in which the British public is investing in so wildly just now. That the kaffir bubble will burst and cata-

strophe follow, few people doubt save those who are reck-
lessly plunging.

The suicide of Barney Barnato has caused a sensation in
financial circles. His office here was besieged this morning
by hundreds of eager inquirers. Throgmorton Street was
filled with excited crowds of bickers discussing the news.
The market as a result was depressed and fractionally lower.
The Pall Mall Gazette says he was mentally unwell for three
months and had been under constant surveillance.

The London St James's Gazette, June 16, 1897

IT IS SAID THAT BARNEY was once upon a time not only a
professional boxer, but, like his brother Harry, thought of
making his fortune as a professor of *legerdemain* - a juggler.
However that may be, I can think of no comparison for his
profession of financier more apt than that of the juggler
who spins plates at the fair. His companies, his multifarious
interests, are his plates and he must keep them all spinning;
and how difficult it is to avoid a smash, how alert the juggler
must be to spring from one to the other, giving a dexterous
twist first to this plate and then to that and keep them all
going lest they knock one another down - the cleverness
necessary for this even the non-financial brain can compre-
hend. When one remembers further that when keeping
financial schemes going there are always people around
whose one endeavour it is to knock down the plates, and
who must be combated or overreached, it is easy to understand the tremendous mental strain involved. Uneasy lies
the head of the financier! No wonder if he loses it
sometimes.

The Salt Lake Tribune, June 15, 1897

THE LATE BARNEY BARNATO was in many respects the most remarkable speculator of the century. Of all the English men who have taken part in the development of South Africa, two only have secured a worldwide reputation. These are Cecil Rhodes and Barnett Isaacs, more often and less respectfully, Barney Barnato styled.

9

PAUL REUTER (JULY 21, 1816 – FEBRUARY 25, 1899)

THE TIMES OF INDIA, FEBRUARY 27, 1899

*B*aron Paul Julius Reuter, whose death is announced today, was the founder and for many years the head of the great news agency whose ramifications extend over the whole civilized world.

He was born in 1816, and, according to *Men and Women of the Time*, he was connected with the electric telegraph system from its earliest establishment. The practical working of the telegraph, in 1849, between Aix-la-Chapelle and Berlin - the first section open to the public - convinced him that a new era in correspondence had arisen, and in the former town he established the first centre of an organisation for collecting and transmitting telegraphic news.

As the various telegraph lines were opened in succession, they were made subservient to his system, and when the cable between Calais and Dover was laid in 1851, Mr Reuter, who had become a naturalised British subject, transferred his chief office to London. Previous to the opening of his office, the leading London papers had furnished the public with scanty and incomplete intelligence, which was reproduced by the rest of the Press, and Mr Reuter, to remedy this defect, established agencies in all parts of the world, to supply him with news, since which time the British Press has contained a daily record of the latest important events connected with politics, commerce and science.

The system which he adopted of supplying all the papers indiscriminately with the same intelligence has greatly contributed to the development of the Penny Press. A similar organisation has been inaugurated by Mr Reuter in America, India, China, Australia, and all the Continental States. It was only by the united contributions of the several branches that the staff of correspondents and the great expenses incidental to the work could be supported, the Press of any single country being insufficient to render such an undertaking possible.

During the Franco-Austrian war, and during the civil war in America, Mr Reuter was fortunate in being the first to publish the most important news, thereby gaining the confidence of the nation and the Press - a confidence which he has maintained by his constant activity. In 1865, Mr Reuter transferred his business to a Limited Liability Company, of which he was the manager, and in the same year he obtained from the Hanoverian Government a concession for the construction of a submarine telegraph line between England and Germany, which enabled a through telegraphic communication to be made between London and the principal towns of Germany.

Mr Reuter also obtained a concession from the French Government for the construction and laying of a cable between France and the United States, which was laid in 1869, and which is worked in conjunction with the Anglo-American Telegraph Company. In 1871, the Duke of Coburg-

Gotha, in recognition of his public services, conferred on him the title of Baron.

Since 1878, the Baron had relinquished his office of managing director of Reuter's Telegram Company, but up to the time of his death still retained a seat on the Board of Directors. Baron Reuter had attracted the attention of the political world, owing to a concession granted to him in 1872 by the Shah of Persia, in virtue of which he had the exclusive privilege of constructing railways, working mines and forests, and making use of all the other natural resources of that country, besides farming the customs. This immense monopoly, which Baron Reuter endeavoured to render subservient to British interests - without, however, excluding other nations - met with difficulties owing to certain intrigues, which difficulties he expected to remove, as her Majesty's Government had interposed in his favour; but the concession was annulled in January 1889, and he received instead the concession of the Imperial Bank of Persia.

The New York Times, February 26, 1899

IN 1851, HAVING ASSOCIATED Baron Emile d'Erlanger with him, Reuter moved his headquarters to London. He had already become a naturalized British citizen. At that time, the London papers had scanty and belated news from foreign countries. Some of them, like *The Times*, employed a fast boat to bring the news that was concentrated in Paris, across the channel from Calais.

It was by a fast boat that *The Times* had got the news of the Battle of Waterloo, and this was still its only means of getting even the most important news from the Continent. Despite this, Reuter received little encouragement from the London papers. His chief employment was furnishing tidings of the Danube wheat movement to Greeks dealing in the London market.

In 1858, Reuter offered to supply to *The Morning Advertiser* and six other papers the news of Europe cheaper and quicker than they were getting it. To show what he could do, he furnished the news free for a fortnight. Even then, *The Times* refused to take the service, but was compelled to do so when its rivals were receiving far more up-to-date news of important events on the Continent. Reuter soon had a monopoly of the news service of the world.

In the civil war in this country, which soon followed, Reuter achieved two great triumphs that more thoroughly established his reputation. These were the transmission of the first news of the seizure of James Mason and John Slidell, Confederate Commissioners to England, and the assassination of Abraham Lincoln.

10

HENRY TATE (MARCH 11, 1819 – DECEMBER 5, 1899)

THE NEW YORK TIMES, DECEMBER 6, 1899

*L*ondon, December 5 - Sir Henry Tate, formerly head of the firm of Henry Tate & Sons, sugar refiners, and donor of the Tate Collection and Picture Gallery, Westminster, is dead.

Sir Henry Tate was the greatest patron of art possessed by England in the latter half of this century. After he had made an immense fortune, he set one aim before himself. That was the recognition in their own country of the merits of the modern English schools of painting. With this idea, Sir Henry acquired a collection of masterpieces of English painters, and, when the terms of his offer to present them to the nation were not agreed to, built the Tate Gallery to house them, and gave both the building and its contents to the people.

Henry Tate was the founder of his own fortunes. He was born at Chorley, Lancashire, 80 years ago. His father was a poor country clergyman, and the poverty of the family made it necessary for the boy to earn his living at an early age. He was apprenticed to a grocer, and at the end of his apprenticeship started in business on his own account. He might have been a country grocer to the end of his days had he not become possessed by the idea that the methods of handling and refining sugar were antiquated and that a fortune awaited anyone who could improve them.

Young Tate therefore went into the refining business in London, and it chanced one day that the inventor of a process for producing dry granulated sugar offered the patent to him. It had been refused by most of the other refiners in London, but Mr Tate give it a trial, with the result that before long the old damp sugar was completely driven out of the market and that the market belonged to Tate. The latter afterward secured another patent, for cutting sugar into cubes, and thereafter became one of the great millionaires of the British metropolis.

Until Mr Tate made his offer of one of the most important collections of English pictures to the nation, he was almost utterly unknown outside of business circles and the suburban society of Streatham. The letter in which he made the offer made him for a time one of the most talked-of men in London. After the gift had been refused, because of the proviso that the nation was to build a home for the pictures, and Mr Tate had thereupon bought the site of the old Millbank Prison and erected a gallery upon it, he was in 1898 made a Baronet. The title descends to his son, William Henry Tate, of Liverpool.

Sir Henry made many other benefactions. It was said to be his rule to give half his income for the public good. The Hahnemann Hospital and Homeopathic Dispensary, in London, were built entirely by him, and so was the library of University College, Liverpool, which cost £16,000. To the same college, he also gave £7,000 for scholarships.

The Westminster Budget, December 8, 1899

SIR HENRY TATE, WHO WAS the son of a clergyman... made his fortune as a sugar refiner in Liverpool, where he became the head of an important firm, Henry Tate & Sons. The special means by which the firm acquired its great wealth in a comparatively short time was the timely introduction of what seemed at first a trifling innovation. At that time, one of the difficulties in connexion with the retail sale of loaf sugar was the awkwardness of cutting the sugar loaves into small pieces ready for domestic use. One day, a man appeared before Sir (then Mr) Henry Tate with an "invention" by means of which sugar could be cut into the small cubes now so generally used. He, the inventor, had been offering his "contrivance" to sugar refiners all over the country, so far without the slightest success or encouragement. Mr Tate, on entertaining into the matter, saw the enormous importance of the invention, bought the instrument, patented it, and his fortune was made.

11

CECIL RHODES (JULY 5, 1853 – MARCH 26, 1902)

THE SCOTSMAN, MARCH 27, 1902

*W*ith regret, but not with surprise, in view of the grave character of the bulletins telegraphed from Cape Town daily during the past fortnight, the announcement will be received of the death of Mr Cecil Rhodes. Mr Rhodes passed away at his temporary residence on the shore at Muizenberg, near Cape Town, at about six o'clock last evening. He was suffering from angina pectoris.

Cecil John Rhodes, the fifth son of the Rev Francis W. Rhodes, vicar of Bishop's Stortford, was born on July 5, 1853. He received his early education at the Grammar School of Bishop's Stortford, which his father had resuscitated and reorganised. From the day that he entered the school till he left it in 1869, he exhibited talents of an exceptional nature, and those prominent characteristics which distinguished him in later years. In the following year, and while yet undecided as to a profession, though his name had been entered at Oriel College, Oxford, young Rhodes was seized with a somewhat serious affection of the lungs, and it was decided that he should visit his eldest brother, Herbert, at that time a cotton-planter in Southern Natal.

On September 1, 1870, he first set foot in that country, in which he was destined to build up a brilliant career. Diamonds had been discovered near the Orange River three years before, and Cape Colony was just then entering on a period of great commercial prosperity. First Herbert, and in turn Cecil determined to try their fortune at the diamond digging, and the two young men set to work on a "claim" at Colesberg Kopje. But no great success attended this first venture.

Having recovered his health, Cecil returned to England, and matriculated at Oxford in 1873. He made it a habit, however, at the end of every summer session of the University to return to the diamond fields at the Cape, with the object mainly of avoiding the rigours of the English winter, under which it was feared his health might again break down. As a matter of fact, the second of these journeys to the Cape was occasioned by his having caught a severe cold while rowing at the University, and but for the invigorating air of Kimberley, to which he returned, he might never have recovered. This, however, did not prevent him from pursuing his studies, and in 1881 he took his BA and MA degrees.

As to his University career, the Rev A.G. Butler, a tutor at Oxford in Mr Rhodes' University days, writes: "Much of his reading was carried on in out-of-the-way places and on board steamers, and it is not a little remarkable how he got at the heart of subject which many fail in reaching. In an earlier part of his college career, Rhodes was once reported to his college dean as not coming to lectures properly. C.R. defended himself by stating that the lecture was at a very early hour, which did not suit him. Then, on being pressed with the difficulty of getting through his examination without lectures, he replied, 'Oh. I promise you I'll manage it. Leave me alone, and I shall pull through.' Rhodes' career at Oxford was uneventful. He belonged to a set of men like himself, not caring for distinctions in the schools, and not working for them, but of refined tastes, dining and living for the most part together, and doubtless discussing passing events in life and politics with interest and ability."

"It is no use having big ideas," Mr Rhodes once remarked to General Gordon, "if one has not the money to carry them out." He, indeed, had a big idea - nothing short of the federation of the States of South Africa under British control, and the extension of the British Empire northwards, through Africa - and accordingly with that perseverance and dogged determination which he had shown from the first, he devoted himself to the task of amassing that large capital which obtained for him the designation of "The Diamond King".

Originally, the laws controlling the diamond fields enacted that no more than one claim should be held by one man, but in 1874 they were revised, to the effect that a person could hold 10 claims. Shortly thereafter this restriction was abolished, and one man could, on certain conditions, hold an indefinite number of claims. Mr Rhodes now saw his opportunity, and was quick to take advantage of it, for he bought up nine of the most promising claims in the neighbourhood of Kimberley. It was at this time that he formed friendships with Mr C.D. Rudd (who afterwards became his partner in many speculations), Mr James Rochefort Maguire, Mr Alfred Beit, and Dr L.S. Jameson. Very soon, Mr Rhodes came to be regarded as one of the ablest speculators in claims in and around Kimberley. Everything he touched seemed to turn out well.

In 1880, the scheme for the amalgamation into one great corporation of all the diamond mines around Kimberley was set on foot, and after several years of hard work on the part of Mr Rhodes, the amalgamation was accomplished, and the threatened glut in the diamond market thereby avoided. Sticking to his original idea with great tenacity of purpose, Mr Rhodes now saw his efforts carried to a successful issue, and the diamond industry put under the control of the De Beers Consolidated Mines (Limited.). In acquiring the diamond monopoly in Cape Colony, Mr Rhodes and those interested in the De Beers mine had a keen fight with Barney Barnato and the others who dominated the Kimberley mine.

Barnato's object was so to regulate the output of diamonds as to obtain as large dividends as possible for his shareholders; but Rhodes viewed the control of the diamond mines as a means for enabling him to obtain ample funds for the purpose of developing his scheme of British expansion towards the Zambezi. By buying up all the shares of the French company in the market, Rhodes finally triumphed over his rivals, and established the great diamond monopoly of the De Beers Consolidated Mines.

In 1880, when Griqualand West had been formally annexed to Cape Colony, Mr Rhodes was elected a member of the Cape Assembly for the district of Barkly West, a constituency which he continued to represent until his death. He made his first speech in the House of Assembly on April 19, 1881, when he was not quite 28 years of age, and three months after The Battle of Majuba. The subject of the speech was the attempted general disarmament of the Basutos, to which Mr Rhodes was strongly opposed. He recognised that, without their weapons, the tribes dwelling on the frontier were incapable of defending themselves against Boer aggression. At the close of the Basuto War, Mr Rhodes was appointed a member of the Commission of the Cape Parliament to proceed to Basutoland to decide what compensation was to be paid to those natives who had remained loyal to the Cape during the revolt, and had suffered in consequence. It was while serving on this Commission that he met General Gordon, who had proceeded to Basutoland to arrange conditions of peace. Gordon from the first was greatly attracted by Rhodes' personality, and the two men, so dissimilar in many respects, but at one in their intense patriotism, became great friends.

When the labours of the Commission were completed, and Rhodes was preparing to return to Kimberley to superintend the working of his diamond mines, Gordon pressed him to stay and assist in the work of pacifying the Basutos and resettling the country; but Rhodes, though with much reluctance, declined the invitation.

Once he had fairly entered on his political career, Mr Rhodes set about the attainment of

his great object - the expansion and consolidation of the British Empire in South Africa. In the House of Assembly, he was immediately recognised as a man of great ability, and to the many matters of importance at that time occupying the attention of the House, he applied himself assiduously. To the proposal to introduce Dutch into the House as the official language side by side with English, Mr Rhodes was opposed, and he seconded an amendment to defer consideration of the matter, not because he had any objection to

Dutch-speaking members being allowed to address the House in their own tongue, but he desired to have an assurance from the Dutch inhabitants of the colony generally that they were anxious for change. While prepared to give the Dutch the same freedom that he claimed for the British, he expected the Dutch on their part to act in the same manner. Though by no means a polished orator, he was always listened to both in and out of the House, and he soon assumed the position of spokesman for Kimberley and district.

One of the earliest matters to which he gave his attention was the question of the boundaries of Griqualand West, which he believed to be closely associated with the object which had led him to enter upon a political career. A Commission was appointed, of which he himself was a member, and it was found that some 70 farms had been unwittingly included in the territory of Griqualand which belonged to the independent chief Mankoroane, these farms being occupied entirely by Boers from the Transvaal, emissaries of President Paul Kruger, sent with the object of seizing the trade route from Cape Colony to the interior. Mr Rhodes determined to keep this route open, and obtained from Mankoroane a formal cession of the territory. The House, however, refused to ratify the concession, and, though Mr Rhodes subsequently obtained the consent of the Imperial Government to a Protectorate being established over the territory in question, on condition that the Cape Government paid one-half of the annual sum necessary for its administration, the Cape Government finally declined to bear any share of the cost of administration, and Mr Rhodes retired to Kimberley disgusted with the short-sighted policy of his colleagues, as he seemed to fear that the Boers were now destined to become the paramount power in South Africa.

For a time thereafter, Mr Rhodes dropped politics, and devoted himself to forwarding the amalgamation movement among the diamond companies. But, on the recommendation of the High Commissioner, the late Lord Derby, then Colonial Secretary, advised the Government to agree to the Protectorate being established, and Mr Rhodes gained what he had battled for so long - the trade route from Cape Colony to the Zambezi.

Unfortunately, some difficulty arose between Mr John Mackenzie, who had been appointed Deputy Commissioner of the newly established Protectorate, and a section of the Boers at Rooigrond, who had directed several attacks upon Montshioa, with the knowledge, it was believed, of President Kruger and the Transvaal Government. The issue of the proclamation by Mr Mackenzie, declaring the whole land in Rooigrond and Stellaland to be the property of the British Government, only served to add fuel to the fire, and for a time it seemed as though all the work accomplished by Mr Rhodes would be set at naught.

The outlook for Bechuanaland was gloomy enough, but, with that energetic spirit and indomitable pluck of the man, Mr Rhodes determined to make one last effort to prevent Bechuanaland passing under the control of the Transvaal. Mr Mackenzie having been recalled to Cape Town, Mr Rhodes went north as Deputy Commissioner of the Bechuanaland Protectorate. He found the situation anything but reassuring. "A pretty kettle of fish" was how he described it.

Supported by a large commando from the Transvaal, the President of the Stellaland Republic was stationed on the banks of the Hartz river, and the Boers of the Rooigrond were still ravaging the country of the chief Montshioa. In short, the British Protectorate was treated with contempt. Rhodes did not falter. Unarmed and alone, and as though unconscious of danger, he sought the camp of the Stellalanders, where he met with Groot Adriaan de la Rey. At the present moment, when the name of the Boer Commandant is constantly before the public, it is interesting to recall what took place at that meeting.

Strolling over to De la Rey's tent one morning, Mr Rhodes calmly invited himself to breakfast. The unexpected visitor was made welcome, but while breakfast was being got ready, De la Rey turned to Rhodes with the ominous remark, "Blood must flow". Rhodes to all appearance remained quite unconcerned, and cooly retorted, "Give me my breakfast, and we will talk about blood afterwards." In the end, De la Rey was won over to Rhodes' way of thinking. Rhodes stayed with De la Rey for a week, and became godfather to his grandchild, and in the end they made a settlement. "Those who were serving under Gert van Niekerk and De la Rey," said Mr Rhodes afterwards, "got their farms, and I secured the government of the country for Her Majesty, which I believe was the right policy, and so both sides were satisfied."

But even yet the difficulties were not ended. General Piet Joubert is said to have urged the Boers of Rooigrond to persist in their defiant attitude, and all hope of bringing about a peaceful settlement was abandoned when President Kruger issued his proclamation annexing Bechuanaland to the Transvaal. A military force set up under the command of Sir Charles Warren brought President Kruger to his senses, and it was arranged that a conference should be held between Mr Kruger, Sir Charles and Mr Rhodes at Fourteen Streams. This was the first occasion on which Mr Rhodes and Mr Kruger were brought face to face. Dr W.J. Leyds, by the way, accompanied Mr Kruger at this meeting, which ended in his promising to relinquish all further claims to the possession of Bechuanaland, and to recall his proclamation. Mr Rhodes had now finally secured for Great Britain the trade route from Cape Colony to the north.

It was while deeply immersed in his schemes for colonial expansion in the north that the Government of Cape Colony suddenly resigned and that Mr Rhodes, as the only man enjoying the confidence of both the British and the Dutch sections of the population, was in 1890 sent for by the High Commissioner, and invited to form a Ministry. With some reluctance, in view of the immensity of the work he had on hand in developing the great territories about to be placed under the control of his company, he accepted the office, having first of all secured from the leaders of the Afrikaner Bond a promise of support on certain conditions.

He was then only 37 years of age. It was his firm intention to weld together into one solid whole the two races, if it was in the bounds of human ability to do so - indeed, this had always been one of his greatest ambitions. Only a man of extraordinary mental and physical faculties could have hoped to overtake the work he had in hand, for, in addition to the duties of Premier, he was the managing director of the newly established Chartered Company, with virtually the whole responsibility of the colonisation and development of Matabeleland on his shoulders.

Amid all his other duties, however, Mr Rhodes found time to push his scheme for a united South Africa under the British flag, successive steps in the development of this scheme being a railway union, a Customs union, and a united policy for the government of the native races.

In the early part of 1891, there was a proposed great trek of the Boers from the Lydenburg district of the Transvaal to the north of the Limpopo, for the purpose of establishing a new Boer Republic. Mr Rhodes protested against this trek, but these protests were ignored by Kruger, and Rhodes quickly moved down all available police of the Chartered Company to the river, where they were joined by hastily enrolled bodies of settlers, and barred the crossing of the trekkers. Mr Rhodes, pursuing the same course which he had done with the Boers of Stellaland seven years before, was prepared to welcome them in Rhodesia and grant them every right and privilege accorded to the British colonists, but they must acknowledge the ultimate supremacy of Great Britain.

The efforts of the Boers to extend the borders of Transvaal northwards were thus frustrated by Mr Rhodes, who made no secret of his purpose to confine the Transvaal to its original boundaries, by encircling it with a zone of British territory. He announced his policy in a speech at Cape Town when he stated in the plainest and most unmistakable language that "no more Boer Republics would be permitted to be set up in South Africa".

In the early part of 1893, the Matabele war broke out, when Lobengula attacked the white settlers in Mashonaland. At this time, the affairs of the South Africa Company were at their lowest ebb, and the outlook was in every way black. The shares of the Chartered Company were only worth some 10 or 12 shillings, while the capital of the company had been almost entirely expended. Mr Rhodes perceived that it was necessary to make a supreme effort if he was to retain his grip on the country, and he sent Dr Jameson up to Mashonaland as Administrator. He had reduced his police force from 700 men to 40, relying upon a Volunteer force at Salisbury; and immediately afterwards the Matabele attack began. Dr Jameson saw that he must strike a decisive blow at once, and he crossed Shangani River into Matabeleland with a force of 900 men, and after two engagements completely broke the power of the Matabele.

Before Dr Jameson's force of Volunteers had been disbanded, Mr Rhodes had reached Matabeleland, and in a short speech thanking the men, he spoke in bitter terms of the cruel slanders which a small but extremely noisy minority at home had seen fit to utter against them. "You would have thought," he said, "that the English would have been satisfied. On the contrary, you have been called free-booting marauders, bloodthirsty murderers and so forth. I know this has not been by the people of England as a whole, but only a section of them. I am as loyal an Englishman as possibly can be, but I cannot help saying that it is such conduct as this that alienated colonists from the mother country. We ask for nothing, for neither men nor money, and still a certain portion vilify us. There are no people more loyal than the colonists in South Africa, but continued misrepresentation will alienate the most loyal."

The leading incidents of the Jameson Raid, in the closing hours of 1895, which followed upon the Johannesburg agitation on account of the Uitlanders' grievances, are still fresh in public recollection. At the official inquiry into the raid by the Committee appointed by the Government, Mr Rhodes was examined at great length, and while expressing his entire sympathy with the position of the Uitlanders in the Transvaal, and his desire to see their grievances redressed, for which purpose he assisted the movement in Johannesburg with his purse and influence, he emphatically asserted that Dr Jameson made his famous march without his authority. But he admitted that in all his actions he was greatly influenced by his belief that the policy of the Transvaal Government was to introduce the influence of another foreign Power into the already complicated system of South Africa, and thereby render more difficult in the future the closer union of the different states. The Committee, among other things, came to the conclusion that Mr Rhodes should have been careful to abstain from such a course of action as that which he adopted.

"Whatever justifications," they continued, "there might have been for action on the part of the people of Johannesburg, there was none, for the conduct of a person in Mr Rhodes' position, in subsidising, organising and stimulating an armed insurrection against the Government of the South African republic, and employing the forces and resources of the Chartered Company to support such a revolution. Although Dr Jameson 'went in' without Mr Rhodes' authority, it was always part of the plan that these forces should be used in the Transvaal in support of an insurrection. Nothing could justify such a use of force and Mr Rhodes' heavy responsibility remains, although Dr Jameson at the last moment invaded the Transvaal without his direct sanction. Such a policy once embarked upon invariably involved Mr Rhodes in grave breaches of duty to those whom he owed allegiance. He deceived the High Commissioner representing the Imperial Government, he concealed his views from his colleagues in the Colonial Ministry, and from the Board of the British South African Company, and led his subordinates to believe that his plans were approved by his superiors."

At the conclusion of his examination before the Raid Committee, in the course of which he was able to show, while under severe cross examination by Sir WIlliam Harcourt, that no money of the Chartered Company was directly employed for the financing of the Jameson raid, Mr

Rhodes, without awaiting the verdict of the Committee, returned to South Africa. On the presentation of the Committee's report to the House of Commons, a somewhat acrimonious debate ensued, in the course of which Mr Chamberlain remarked that however much Mr Rhodes might have failed in his duties as a public man, there was nothing in the whole affair which redounded to his private dishonour.

The Matabele Rebellion of 1896 again sent Mr Rhodes upcountry, where an incident occurred which goes far to disprove the belief entertained in some quarters that he was hated by the Dutch in South Africa. It was always part of his settled policy to conciliate the Dutch-speaking population, and when the column to which he was attached to reached Enkeldoorn, the trek Boers from the Transvaal gave him quite an ovation, fired salutes in his honour, and presented him with an address of welcome, which he treasured as one of his most cherished possessions. The Boers begged him to act towards them as a "father". "Even as Oom Paul Kruger has acted in the light of a father to the Boers of the Transvaal, so we would request you to act as a father to those Boers who have made their home in Rhodesia."

Mr Rhodes's response took the form of a large sum out of his private purse towards indemnifying the Boers of Enkeldoorn for the losses they had sustained through the rising of the Matabele and the destruction of their cattle by the rinderpest. The first collision between the force and the Matabele at Makalaka Kop showed that the Matabele were not disposed to yield without a struggle. In a pitched battle between the Salisbury column and the Matabele in the Mavin district on May 9, Mr Rhodes gave a striking exhibition of that intrepidity which afterwards led him to take his unarmed expedition to the Matoppo Hills, the stronghold of the rebels, in order to discuss terms of peace - one of the most dramatic events of his by no means uneventful career. There were only three white men with Rhodes, two friendly natives being taken as guides. He carried nothing more deadly than a small riding whip. It was a perilous undertaking, which few men would have dared to attempt, for the least false step would have meant the annihilation of the little party. It is unnecessary to repeat here all that occurred at that memorable palaver. Suffice it to say that Rhodes, as though by a miracle, succeeded in bringing the rebellion to an end, and in rescuing the British South African Company from ruin.

With the "Cape-to-Cairo Railway" the name of Cecil Rhodes will always be closely identified. The dream of an "all-red" railway line from the south to the north of Africa seized hold of his imagination in the early days of his political career, and the more he dwelt upon it the greater seemed to be his determination to carry it out. He declined to listen to the proposal of Afrikaner Bond that Kimberley should remain the northern terminus of the railway, and the next section, from Kimberley to Mafeking, was built. Beyond Kimberley, the Cape Legislature refused to go, but by forming the Bechuanaland Railway Company, Rhodes carried the line northwards, and, amid a scene of great popular rejoicing, it was formally opened to Bulawayo on November 4, 1897.

The junction of German East Africa and Congo Free State to the north of Lake Tanganyika put an end to his idea of an "all-red" railway across Africa, and it was, therefore, necessary to traverse German or Congo Free State territory. Believing that the better country was on the German side, Mr Rhodes, in order to further his object, set out on a visit to Germany, where he was cordially received by the Emperor, with whom he had several interviews, the outcome of which was that the Kaiser assented to the telegraph system passing through the German colonies. As regards the railway, that was left in abeyance.

What really led to this visit to Germany was the failure of the negotiations between Mr Rhodes and the Imperial Government as to the guarantee he had asked with reference to the further extension of the railway. He was determined to push on with the scheme northwards from Bulawayo, and towards this end, he got the Rhodesian and mining land companies which owned property in the neighbourhood of the route to take up debentures - half a million being subscribed almost immediately. The estimated cost of building this 750-mile section to Lake Tanganyika was £3,000,000. The transcontinental telegraph project across the plateau of British Central Africa and onward to the Nile, which at the present rate of progress is expected to be in working order by the end of 1903, was another of his great projects. The cost of building the whole line, by which Mr Rhodes estimated a saving to the public of 1s 3d for every word telegraphed, he set down at £100 per mile.

When the negotiations which led up to the present war were in progress between Mr Joseph Chamberlain and President Kruger, Mr Rhodes was careful not to interfere. "I made a mistake with regard to the Transvaal once," he said, "and that was quite enough for me. No one will be able to say if things go wrong 'That Rhodes is in it again!'"

On war being declared by the Republics, he felt there was no further need for remaining inactive, and in view of the enormous interests he had in Kimberley, he set off to the diamond town, which he rightly guessed would be one of the first objectives of the Boer commandos. He reached Kimberley by the last train to enter the town before the commencement of the siege, after narrowly escaping capture. The part he took in the defence of the town and the many ways in which he assisted the military authorities are so fresh in the public minds that they need not be repeated here.

On the relief of Kimberley, Mr Rhodes returned to Groote Schuur. His active interest in the war was now at an end, but, needless to say, down to the day of his death, he followed each turn in the hostilities with the greatest interest.

The Colossus of South Africa, as he has been appropriately styled, Mr Rhodes has been the most conspicuous figure in that part of the Empire from the origination of the Chartered Company down to the eve of the war. His name was always one to conjure with, and his influence, on whichever side it was thrown, never failed to make itself felt. Although not always in a majority in the Cape Parliament, his was ever a powerful personality which could command support where others would fail to obtain it. He was a man of great force of character and of infinite resource, and before his indomitable will and persevering nature, no obstacle, however formidable, seemed insuperable in the attainment of the object on which he had set his heart.

He was largely instrumental in retaining Bechuanaland in British hands, to the exclusion of the Boers, and he saw the settlement of the vast territory of Rhodesia, fittingly named after him. His great Cape to Cairo scheme has not yet been realised, but he broached a project which is being brought nearer of accomplishment, and the annexation of the South African Republics and their future development will do much to help it on.

From the early days of his work on the diamond fields at Kimberley, he cherished the dream of winning the north and the whole backbone of Africa for England. He saw from the first that two instruments were needed to realise his dream - political power and financial power. These he succeeded in gaining, and in a remarkable degree he won the confidence and support of the most honourable and able of the South African capitalists.

He was also successful in saving for Britain the immense hinterland up to Lake Tanganyika, and he brought to the solution of the problems and difficulties with which he had to deal a singular combination of business ability, tenacity of purpose, foresight, and sagacious judgement. More than any other man, he made history in South Africa, and our possession of Rhodesia and the regions north of the Zambezi, is directly due to the great work of Mr Rhodes.

On a visit to England in 1899, the University of Oxford conferred on Mr Rhodes the honorary degree of D.C.L. (Doctor of Civil Law) in 1891, while visiting England in order to lay before the Imperial Government several important points with regard to the settlement of Mashonaland, Mr Rhodes was honoured with a command to dine with Queen Victoria, and it is said that he retained very pleasant memories of the way in which her late Majesty received him, and of the keen interest she showed in the development of Mashonaland under the British flag, of the diamond mines at Kimberley, and of the manner in which stones were obtained and prepared for the market. Mr Rhodes was created a member of the Privy Council in February 1895.

It will be remembered that during his visit to England in 1891, Mr Rhodes gave Charles Stewart Parnell £10,000 in aid of the cause of Home Rule for Ireland. He seemed to think, as he explained some time afterwards, that he saw in that policy the germ of Imperial Federation, by which at some future time every self-governing colony and dependency should be represented at Westminster; but he was entirely opposed to the policy of withdrawing the Irish representatives from the Imperial Parliament. Within the past year, there was considerable controversy as to the conditions under which Mr Rhodes had presented £5,000 to the funds of the Liberal Party. These were the only intimate connections which Mr Rhodes had with politics in this country.

Mr Rhodes was not a frequent or a copious speaker, but his utterances were always clearly expressed, and his meaning was never left in doubt. He seldom referred to his own personality or to the part which he himself played in the great undertakings with which he was associated, but the following passages, addressed to his constituents at Barkly West in October 1888, have a special interest:

"There have been many things invented respecting my career, and I have been told that my object is to obtain a seat in the English Parliament, but, of course, I take no heed of these rumours, as there is no truth in them. It is my intention to remain attached to Cape politics, for I take a great interest in them; and I tell you candidly that I have not the slightest idea of quitting South Africa for any other country. Here I can do something, but were I to go to England as a politician I should be lost in obscurity. I have been told that my desire is to enter the English Parliament and that my contribution to the Parnell Fund was with this object. I have the presumption to say that I believe I could at any time obtain a seat in the English Parliament without paying Mr Parnell £10,000, and that if I ever stood for the English Parliament I should not stand for an Irish constituency. I gave Mr Parnell's cause £10,000 because in it I believed lies the key of the Federal system on the basis of perfect Home Rule in every part of the Empire."

The recreations of this many-sided man are thus

recorded: "Kept the drag at Oxford; rides daily for two hours at 6am; reads chiefly the classics, of which he has fine collection, with a separate library of typewritten translations executed specially for him; Froude and Carlyle he admires universally; favourite reading, biography and history; knows Gibbon almost by heart; favourite work of fiction *Vanity Fair,* which he admires more than any other single work in literature; collects old furniture, china, and curios generally, with a preference for anything Dutch; has a Sir Joshua Reynolds; fond of nearly all old fashions; fond of old things, particularly of old oak chests; goes in greatly for gardening, especially rose-culture; good pyramid player; a fair shot; has a menagerie on Table Mountain, and visits his lions there every day when he can; his zebras, ostriches, and buck of all kinds are not caged, but run wild in huge enclosed tracts of the mountain side."

The New York Times, March 27, 1902

CECIL RHODES HAS BEEN variously described. He has been called "the Napoleon of Africa", "the modern Caesar", "the most farsighted statesman of his age". The Boers termed him "the murderer". His career, if set forth in a romance, would be criticized as absurdly impossible. He had absolutely nothing in his favor at the start - neither riches, nor influence, nor even health...

...Mr Rhodes showed his qualities by his choice of assistants as by anything else. Men who most people regarded as incompetents and failures were taken up by him and made millionaires. Among them were Barney Barnato and Henry J. King. The only mine owner who went into the scheme on an equality with Rhodes was Alfred Beit, now said to be the richest man in the world. De Beers is an amalgamation of the Dutoitspan, the Central, the Kimberley, and the De Beers companies. A year after it was formed, it had succeeded, by limiting production, in doubling the price of stones in all the great markets. Rhodes then became known as the "Diamond King".

JAMSETJI TATA (MARCH 3, 1839 – MAY 19, 1904)

THE TIMES OF INDIA, MAY 20, 1904

We much regret to announce the death of Mr Jamsetji Nusserwanji Tata, the well-known mill-owner and millionaire of Bombay, which took place yesterday at Nauheim, a watering place in Germany, where he was taken for a change of air. Mr Tata had been for some time past in indifferent health, and he accordingly left Bombay under medical advice for Egypt in January last. He first went to Cairo, and then proceeded to Naples and visited other cities on the continent, and eventually went to Vienna, where he remained under medical treatment.

While he was at Vienna, he sent for Dr Rao, his family physician in Bombay, who immediately repaired to that place, and sent information, by wire last week, to members of Mr Tata's family to say that Mr Jamsetji's condition was anything but satisfactory. On Saturday last, a telegram was received in Bombay that Mr Tata had removed to Nauheim and afterwards another message that his strength was failing. News was again received yesterday morning that Mr Tata was getting worse and at about 3.30pm the intelligence of his death was wired to members of his family in Bombay.

The news spread quickly in the city, and by 5pm a large number of Parsis assembled at the Tata's mansion to offer their condolences to Mr Ratan J. Tata, the younger of the two sons of the deceased gentleman.

Mr Dorab, the eldest son, and Mrs Dorab had been with Mr Jamsetji ever since he went to Europe for a change. Latterly, Mr Ratan D. Tata, a nephew of the deceased gentleman, also joined the party in Vienna, and it is a great consolation to the relations and friends of Mr Tata in Bombay that at the time of his death he was surrounded by members of his family and his family physician, in whom Mr Tata had great confidence. Mr Ratan Tata has been apprised that the body of Mr Tata will be removed to London as soon as practicable, and that it will be interred in the Parsee cemetery near Woking.

Born at Navsari, a town in Gujarat, in the year 1839, Mr Tata was at the time of his death about 65 years of age. He was brought to Bombay when he was only 13 years old, and after he had received a scholastic education, he entered the Elphinstone College, where he had a course of study for four years, and when he attained the age of 19, he joined his father's firm of commissariat contractors. Mr Nusserwanji Tata, the father of Mr Jamsetji, had had a chequered career. He was once favoured by fortune, but he lost all during the share mania of the early sixties. During the Abyssinian expedition, the Government contractors were able to amass large fortunes, and old Mr Nusserwanji again became a wealthy man. Mr Nusserwanji was a staunch Zoroastrian, and he spent lakhs of rupees on the construction of fire-temples and towers-of-silence, and his charities were more or less confined to his own co-religionists.

Shortly after having joined his father's firm, Mr Jamsetji left Bombay for China, where he laid the foundations of a mercantile firm, which grew with the growth of time, and was conducted under the name and style of Messrs Tata and Co, with branches in Japan, Hong Kong, Shanghai, Paris and New York.

The firm prospered under his guidance and control, and when he returned from China to Bombay, he made up his mind to proceed to Europe for the purpose of establishing an Indian Bank in London, but the financial crash that occurred in Bombay at the time prevented him from carrying out the project. He visited England all the same, and the result was that on his return to Bombay, he purchased the Chinchpokli Oil Mill, which he converted into a spinning and weaving concern called the Alexandra Mills, and having worked it at a profit sold it to the late Mr Kessowji Naik on advantageous terms. The success he had met with in connection with the mill industry induced him to pay a second visit to England with the object of studying the conditions of the cotton mill industry in Lancashire, and the knowledge he acquired there and in other manufacturing towns of England stood him in good stead when he returned to Bombay to start a cotton mill on a larger scale. He looked at the project from all points of view, and travelled all over India to find out where the venture would best succeed.

After a protracted and minute inquiry, Nagpur was at last fixed as a central place where a large cotton mill was to be erected. Foundations were laid, and on January 1, 1877, the day on which her Majesty the late Queen Victoria was declared Empress of India, the now world-renowned Empress Mills were opened and Mr Tata was justly called a captain of the mill industry in India. Speaking at the opening of a new spinning shed at the Nagpur Mills 18 years later, Mr Tata said he did not claim to be more unselfish, more generous or more philanthropic than other people. But he did claim that the mills were started on sound and straightforward principles. He considered the interests of the shareholders as his own, and the welfare of his employees as the surest foundation of his prosperity. He further stated at the time that the management of the Empress Mills set their face strenuously against the system of the quarter anna commission, which had brought many a Bombay mill to the brink of ruin. At the time, the spinning department was further extended and opened, Mr Tata had working under his management over one lakh [100,000] of spindles and nearly 2,500 looms.

Encouraged by the phenomenal success of the Empress Mills, Mr Tata thought of Pondicherry as a suitable site for another mill conducted on the same principles as the former. The main object was to find a market for Indian manufactured goods in French colonies without having to pay the prohibitive tariffs imposed by their fiscal system. A company was actually formed, but instead of building a new mill at Pondicherry, they preferred to buy up the Dharamsi Mill at Kurla, which is now known as the Svadeshi Mill, and which, though it did not in any way come up to the Empress Mills, has been worked with greater success than many of the Bombay mills.

The most important direction in which Mr Tata contributed to the development of the mill industry was the production of superior kinds of woven goods, which found an extensive sale in the country. It was in connection with this important departure that Mr Tata conceived the idea of establishing his own agencies and shops in different towns - a practice which has since been followed by others.

The idea of spinning finer counts naturally gave birth to the idea of growing long-staple cotton in the country. The possibility of growing Egyptian cotton in India was one of the many subjects on which Mr Tata was strongly at variance with Government officials. He proposed to conduct certain experiments with Egyptian cotton in certain localities where the best varieties of cotton were produced; but the chief difficulties he encountered were those of irrigation and the excessive dryness of the air in places removed from the sea. Mr Tata personally studied the conditions of the growth of the plant in its native home, and it may be mentioned that experiments with Egyptian cotton carried on at the Government Farm at Nagpur have yielded promising results.

It was with the object of supporting and promoting the mill industry of Bombay that Mr Tata, combined with the premier Japanese Steamship Company, waged a war of freights with the P&O Company, the Austrian Lloyd's and the Italian Rubattino Companies, who monopolised the freight for the carriage of cotton to China and Japan, with the result that the triple alliance had to reduce the freight from Bombay to Japan to one rupee per ton. Mr Tata protested in a pamphlet, which was circulated in many parts of the world, against the iniquity of a company subsidised heavily from Indian revenues using that very subsidy to make up for the loss involved in the ruinous competitive rate to which they had reduced their charges, and appealed to the British to create a strong public opinion in favour of his cause. The war of freights, which resulted in some sort of a compromise, cost Mr Tata about two lakhs of rupees [200,000].

Mr Tata was, as is well-known, largely interested in building operations in Bombay and elsewhere, and the correspondence he had with the local Government in respect of building sites in Salsette attracted public attention at the time. He was chiefly instrumental in introducing the silk industry after the Japanese method in Mysore.

It is the irony of fate that Mr Tata should have died just when one of the noblest of his enterprises, and one in which he ever betrayed the keenest interest, should be rapidly approaching completion. The Taj Mahal Hotel, whose lofty dome and splendid facade dominate the harbour, is the creation of Mr Tata's fertile brain; the solid magnificence with which it has been executed in every part is the fruit of his own far-sighted liberality. We should entirely misread Mr Tata's character if we concluded that the hotel was to him a mere commercial venture. A widely travelled man, and a man of cultivated taste, he could not fail to be impressed with the extraordinary deficiencies of the Indian hotel system, in Bombay no less than in every other part of the country. He saw that elsewhere hotels filled a very important part in the amenities of social life, and that more particularly in the complex society of the East they played a role which no other institution could fill.

He determined that Bombay should have a hotel second to none east of Suez, and that it should set an example which should react throughout India in removing one of the greatest hindrances to agreeable travel in this country. So he had the plans of his hotel drawn with the sole purpose of securing an entirely worthy building; he spared no expense in the raising of the magnificent superstructure; he equipped it with the latest modern appliances in the way of electric light, fans, lifts, and cold storage apparatus; and he placed at the head of it a "maitre d'hotel" of European reputation.

This he did without looking for any immediate financial return, but content that he should be able to regard his handiwork from every point and find it good, that he should give his city something fully worthy of its architectural magnificence and its unique position as the gateway of India. For interest upon the huge sum he embarked in the enterprise, he was well content to wait. In none of his adventures was Mr Tata's largeness of mind and wise liberality more conspicuous than in this, the creation of his old age; he has endowed the city with a hotel which will make the stranger linger within its gates, and which will prove of incalculable advantage to the dweller in the Presidency. There is something peculiarly saddening in the coincidence that the fixing of the keystone of the noble dome should have preceded by only a few days the death of the man who inspired it.

Mr Tata was a great believer in higher education. Many years ago, he endowed a fund for sending Parsi youths to England for purposes of study. In the year 1894, the benefits of the fund were thrown open to all castes. The operations of the fund have been highly successful. The proposed Research University was, however, his greatest educational scheme. The scheme and the endowment proposed were announced on September 28, 1898. But the idea was born in Mr Tata's mind at least two years earlier, and educational experts in Europe had been consulted beforehand in person by Mr B.J. Padshaw, the Honorary Secretary. The scheme has undergone alterations since its inception, and the eminent scientist Professor William Ramsay's report finally fixes it as mainly an institution for carrying on chemical research. Mr Tata had made up his mind not to start the institute on a financial basis less than 14,000 to 15,000 pounds a year.

Negotiations between the committee appointed by Mr Tata, and the Government of India and the Maharaja of Mysore are not yet quite completed. It is highly probable that the scheme will sooner or later come into force, but in case it did not, it was Mr Tata's intention to divert his own fund to another Trust, which would enable students to go to Europe to qualify for the Indian Civil and other services, and for the electrical and engineering professions, until such time as it became possible, with the proper aid of Government, to start the Research Institute as originally planned.

In the latter eighties, Mr Tata had an important share in experiments carried on in the Central Provinces in smelting iron ore with local coal. He was not, however, to set his hand to the plough and then turn back. Undeterred by official indifference and circumlocution, he kept the project in mind, and referred to scientific experts some of the practical difficulties encountered by him. On the occasion of one of his recent visits to England, he mentioned the project in the course of conversation to Lord George Hamilton. The interest of the then Secretary of State was at once aroused, and he pressed Mr Tata to take it up vigorously, and urged him to be mindful of the patriotic obligation he was under, as the most enterprising of Indian businessmen, to contribute in every way possible to the industrial development of the country.

On returning to India, Mr Tata found that the obstruction or indifference of the secretariats had been replaced by not merely a readiness, but an eagerness to assist. He confidently believed that when the industry was organized, the Central Provinces would take rank as possessing the most valuable iron deposits in the world. It was estimated that on a capital of about a crore of rupees [10m], an outturn of 300 tons of steel daily could be secured under the most unfavourable circumstances, and a much larger quantity if possible difficulties were overcome. Mr Tata also took steps to revive in the Chanda district of the Central Provinces the working of copper mines believed to have been abandoned a thousand years since. No time was too precious, no cost too great in his eyes to be spent in investigating thoroughly and from all possible points of view the conditions necessary to make a project successful, and he has already spent a lakh and a half of rupees in proving his concessions in the Central Provinces.

By Mr Tata's death, the mill industry of India has lost one of its greatest captains, the Parsis a leading member of their community, and the educated Indians one of their greatest benefactors.

MARSHALL FIELD (AUGUST 18, 1834 – JANUARY 16, 1906)

ity THE NEW YORK TIMES, JANUARY 17, 1906

The mercantile and commercial career of Marshall Field stands as a monument to his industry, perseverance, energy, and faculty for invention. He was rated one of the world's greatest merchants, and in the East and West was accepted as a man of extraordinary business talents. Perhaps the best epitome of the rules of his life is furnished in his own words. He wrote:

"He never gives a note.

He never buys a share of stock on margin.

He is against speculation.

He is no borrower.

He has made it a point not to encumber his business with mortgages.

He does business on a "cash basis".

He tries to sell on shorter time than competitors.

He tries to sell the same grade of goods for a smaller price.

He holds his customers to a strict meeting of their obligations."

He made those rules years ago and never announced

any revision. If any of his great enterprises afterward required the borrowing of money it was never known that he had borrowed it. And Mr Field did more than make himself rich. He made his associates rich. One man after another has stepped out of the house of Marshall Field & Co and retired with a fortune. But while others sought ease, Marshall Field, the front of the concern, remained in command till the last.

Mr Field was an upright man. The platform of probity was that upon which he amassed his fortune. He never knew in later years just how much he was worth, so widely were his possessions distributed, and in such various commodities - factories, real estate, industrial concerns, stocks and bonds - did it lie. A total of $150,000,000 is believed by many to be nearer the truth about his wealth than the frequently quoted popular appraisal of $100,000,000.

Although there are larger estates in the country, Mr Field was in 1903 the largest individual taxpayer in the United States. He paid more than $500,000 in Cook County taxes alone, and the estimate of taxes paid in States outside of Illinois was $250,000 more. He paid taxes on $40,000,000 worth of Chicago property, of which $30,000,000 was in real estate. Of two comparatively recent statements made by financial experts, one placed the value of all the Field holdings at $175,000,000 and the other at $125,000,000.

The life story of Marshall Field is that of a farmer's son who went from New England to the West. No sedate proverb ever epitomized a record like that of the Field boy. From a lad in the quiet of a Massachusetts community to a manhood interwoven with every stage of the growth of the City of Chicago, starting when his career began with a population of 50,000, and then developing into a city of

2,000,000. From a clerk in a small dry goods shop to the proprietorship of some of the biggest stores in the world. From nothing to a vast fortune. That is an outline of his career.

No man, in the belief of Mr Field, could divide his energy and succeed. He chose business at the beginning, and kept to it to the end. And his strength was in the power of concentration. He thought about what he did while he was doing it and about nothing else.

Mr Field's first wife died in seclusion several years ago. The interval between September of 1905 and his death yesterday saw his marriage in London on September 5, 1905, to Mrs Delia Spencer Caton, the widow of his neighbor and friend, Arthur Caton; and the death in November last under tragic circumstances of his only son, Marshall Field Jr.

Marshall Field was born August 18, 1834. The first 17 years of his life were spent on the home farm near Conway, Massachusetts. When the boys of the Field household scattered and Marshall and his brother Henry went West, the father and mother moved into Conway and lived there until their deaths. Marshall Field was the third of a family of six children.

His father, John Field, was a typical Yankee. He was what is known as a hard driver, and when at home young Marshall Field lived the hard life of a farmer's boy. When he was six years old, he was sent to the district school. Among his playmates, though a bit younger, was the late William C. Whitney. The elder Mr Whitney was Postmaster of the village. Marshall's brothers and sisters were Chandler, Joel N, Nellie, Henry, and Kate. At the age of 15, he quit school and went to Pittsfield nearby, and engaged as a clerk in a general merchandise house. When the proprietor of this house later heard of Field's success in Chicago, he said:

"Well, I never thought it of him. He was about the greenest looking lad I ever saw when he came to work for me. Though he learned fast, I never thought he'd be a rich man."

After four years of work in the Pittsfield store, Field quit and in 1856 he went to Chicago. He had the savings of his labor, and immediately put them to good advantage. He went to work at once in the wholesale dry goods house of Cooley, Wadsworth & Co. In four years, the clerk was a member of the firm, the year being 1860, civil war already brewing, and prices beginning to rise. It was a good time to start to build a fortune. Mr Field started. The firm meantime had become Cooley, Farwell & Co, and before the war was over, it was Farwell, Field & Co. The fortune had received a good foundation.

In 1805, the firm was re-organized again, becoming Field, Palmer & Leiter, the other partners being Levi Z. Leiter and Potter Palmer. The last-named remained a member of the firm only two years, the firm name then being changed to Field, Leiter & Co, a naming which endured until the present style of Marshall Field & Co was assumed in 1881 on the retirement of Mr Leiter.

At the time of the fire of 1871, the Field house did a business of $8,000,000 a year. The property destroyed by the conflagration was valued at $3,500,000. The insurance collected amounted to $2,500,000, which meant a loss to the firm of an even million.

The Chicago buildings at present occupied by Marshall Field & Co are four in number, so as to give the effect of one. Within the building is a branch Post Office, and, according to the Postmaster of Chicago, it "ranks with cities of the class of Bloomington, Joliet, and Danville, Illinois, East Orange, New Jersey, and Albany, New York. Last year ,there were issued from this station 7,012 domestic and 134 international money orders, amounting to $55,792.86; stamps sold to the amount of $67,501.10, and 2,625 pieces of registered matter were handled". This does not include the mail of the company. The Field delivery system covers an area of 303 square miles.

In all establishments, Marshall Field & Co employs more than 12,000 persons. In the retail store, the number of employees fluctuates, according to the season of the year, from 6,500 to 9,000. In the wholesale establishment and the storehouses, the number ranges from 3,400 to 3,600, the others being employed in the foreign offices.

While building up the drygoods business, which has grown to such mammoth proportions, Mr Field, who was a firm believer in the future of Chicago, invested heavily in real estate, and to the appreciation of this in value he owed much of his wealth.

At the close of the World's Fair in 1893, he endowed with $1,000,000 the museum known as the Field Columbian museum, for which a home worth $8,000,000 is shortly to be erected in the heart of the city. He later gave to the University of Chicago land valued at $450,000, to be used for athletic purposes, and a portion of it is known today as Marshall Field. He was extremely charitable in other directions, never failing to contribute to a cause which he knew to be worthy.

Personally, Mr Field was a handsome man, a trifle above medium height, slender, and well proportioned. He was popular socially, although he never mingled in society as the word is generally understood. In his personal tastes and habits, he was quiet and modest. In politics, he never interfered, although he was always ready to aid with time and money any movement looking toward better national or municipal government. He was prominently mentioned as a

Vice Presidential candidate on the Democratic ticket in 1904. He was offered the second place on the ticket several times, but refused to accept it.

Although Mr Field was a Presbyterian in church worship, he early became a financial supporter of the University of Chicago, a Baptist institution. Marshall Field, the athletic grounds of the university, bears his name in token of one of his several gifts. A library which he erected in Conway, Mass., cost $200,000.

Mr Field had never engaged in real estate speculation in this city upon a scale to attract much public attention. His buying had been confined practically to a single operation - the acquisition of the block front on the east side of Fifth Avenue, between Thirtieth and Thirty-first Streets - although it is said that he had owned for a long time one or two properties in the wholesale drygoods district around Worth Street.

Mr Field began buying on Fifth Avenue about 10 or 12 years ago. His purchases, completed in 1894, covered not only the Fifth Avenue part of the block, but also adjoining parcels, until he finally controlled a frontage of 164 feet on Thirtieth Street and 254 feet on Thirty-first Street. The entire property is worth today probably between $3,000,000 and $4,000,000. When Mr Field was getting together this large plot, it was generally supposed that it was his ultimate intention to erect a great dry goods store on the property. This, however, proved not to be the case, for soon after Benjamin Altman made announcement concerning his new enterprise at Fifth Avenue and Thirty-fourth Street, he closed negotiations with Mr Field for a 99-years lease of the block between Thirtieth and Thirty-first Streets.

EDWARD HARRIMAN (C.FEBRUARY 20, 1848 - SEPTEMBER 9, 1909)

THE BOSTON POST, SEPTEMBER 10, 1909

*E*dward Henry Harriman was born February 25, 1848, at Hempstead, Long Island. His father was Orlando Harriman, rector of a small parish on a still smaller salary, which was not paid in full. Mr Harriman was 11 years old when the parish of St John's offered his father a salary of $200 a year, and he accepted it the same night it was offered to him. By this time, there were six children, four boys and two girls. How they managed to exist on $200 a year must have been the secret of the mother. She taught her boys and girls what pride of race meant. The family was a close corporation. If they suffered, they kept it to themselves.

Thus, the future empire builder grew into his teens. He had a common school education, finished off by two years at a school where clergymen's sons received free tuition. But for this provision, there would have been nothing after the common school for Henry Harriman, as he was then called. Towards the end of the '60s, Orlando Harriman inherited a little money. It was not a great sum, but it was enough to permit him to retire from his parish and purchase a home in

Jersey City, and it was from this home that Edward Henry entered Wall Street as a clerk.

He was still small, slight and keenly observant. He made friends readily in those days and cultivated the social side of life, meeting only the best of the young men and those who had social connections. He was not a talkative youth, but he had a keen sense of humor, and he preferred to listen while others did the talking. His eyes were wide open, for he was even then beginning to study the workings of the great money machine which he was one day to control.

When he was 22 years of age, young Harriman suddenly amazed his friends by purchasing a seat on the stock exchange. Where the money came from will never be known. There is a story to the effect that Harriman, youngster though he was, read the market on the Gould-Fisk "corner on gold" and turned his slender savings Into enough money to buy his seat. Another story, and the more probable one, is that he got it from his father's family.

At any rate, in 1870, Edward H. Harriman was a member of the Stock Exchange, and at once began to turn his information into money. It was at a panic time. The crashes of 1871 and 1872 are still remembered. Somewhere in that swirling pit of crazy money, the future master of Wall Street was biding his time, watching men and events and storing his mind with knowledge against the day when he should be powerful enough to use it. Young Harriman was a shrewd trader. He preferred a small profit to a risk. Soon he was spoken of as "a smart young man". In five years, he was a veteran, for he had been through several of the great panics. At 30, with eight years of Wall Street behind him, Harriman had learned the game. He had spent this time in learning the game rather than playing it and he had begun to save a little money and teach it to make more for him.

He was also married. His wife was a Miss Mary Averell, of Rochester, the daughter of a capitalist and a successful railroad man. The marriage was a fortunate one in every way and Mr Harriman's home life was singularly happy.

The years between 1870 and 1880 were stormy ones on the stock exchange, but out of every panic young Harriman emerged a little stronger financially, a little surer of himself and of the men about him, and a little richer in the experience which he was to use so tellingly in after years. He knew the trick of watching a stock until it touched low-water mark and catching it before it began to move upwards once more. In this way, he picked up many a block of stock which afterward became valuable, and in 1880 he was regarded as a capitalist on his own account.

Thirteen years after Mr Harriman entered Wall Street, he took the first step towards what was to be his future field of activity. Stuyvesant Fish, the same man whom he in after years fought so bitterly and deposed from his position at the head of a great railroad, was young Harriman's friend. Stuyvesant Fish became the second vice-president of the Illinois Central. At the same time, E.H. Harriman became a director of the road. Harriman went into railroading as he had gone into Wall Street. He wanted to learn the game and he kept his eyes open. So well did he succeed that when Mr Fish became the president of the road, which was in 1887, Harriman became vice-president.

Mr Harriman had come into his own. Wall Street gave to him a place among the great financiers, but he had yet to demonstrate he was a railroad man. He accepted the opportunity and began to show that with him the control of a railroad stood for good railroading. The Alton had been paying dividends, but at the cost of maintenance, and he began to rebuild the road, a division at a time. Grades were lowered, curves were cut out, bridges rebuilt and new rails laid. The work of reconstruction took three years, but the Alton had been changed to a modern road and the returns justified the outlay. At this time, the newspapers began to call Mr Harriman a "New York capitalist". He was referred to in that way when in 1898 he equipped and sent to Alaska the first expedition to thoroughly investigate the resources of that territory. Mr Harriman saw then the possibilities of that country and the wealth it would bring to the ports of the Pacific for shipment to the East.

It was in 1899 that Mr Harriman became the directing genius of the Union Pacific. His success in reorganizing the Alton brought about his election as chairman of the executive committee of its board of directors. The road had been sold on the foreclosure of the government mortgage, and Mr Harriman began the reorganization of its finances, which provided a future of expansion and consolidation undreamed of by the financiers of that time. From the moment he began to control the destinies of the system and began to build it up, he seemed to see at his feet the control of the commerce from the Pacific coast to the East. But he saw that to develop fully its earning power there would have to be expansion, as well as a complete reconstruction of the parent line. The road had already purchased the Kansas Pacific from Kansas City to Denver, and obtained control of the stock of the Oregon Short Line, which gave it its only outlet to the Pacific coast. Mr Harriman provided the millions, and an army of contractors began to rebuild the road, which was entirely reconstructed in two years, without an interruption of a day's traffic.

While he was rebuilding, he began to plan for another

and a more southerly terminal on the Pacific. The Union Pacific proper ends at Ogden, and the Central Pacific runs from Ogden to San Francisco. The late Collis P Huntington controlled both the Southern Pacific and the Central Pacific, and Mr Harriman went to him with an offer to purchase the latter. Mr Huntington declared he would not sell it and would not let Mr Harriman get in California, his own territory, for years.

Within a week after Mr Huntington had refused to sell the road, it was announced that the Utah & Northern railroad had been incorporated to build from Salt Lake City to San Francisco. Its stock was owned by the Oregon Short Line and Mr Harriman announced that it would be the main line of the Union Pacific from Utah to the coast, and the work had been pushed to the Nevada State line by the summer of 1900. Without the Union Pacific as an eastern outlet, the Central Pacific was a railroad stranded in a wilderness, and Mr Huntington had conceived no counter stroke to the plan evolved by the genius of Mr Harriman when in August he died.

Mr Harriman brought into action that wonderful play of high finance, and in seven months the holdings of Mr Huntington in Southern Pacific and Central Pacific, with those of the Stanford and Crocker interests, were sold to the Union Pacific, which issued bonds for the purchase.

From that day, no man or interest has disputed the rule of Mr Harriman in the Pacific field. With a single stroke, he added 9,621 miles to the Union Pacific system, gained the coveted entrance into San Francisco and became the dominant railroad factor in the territory reaching eastward from that city to the Gulf of Mexico.

With the purchase of the Southern Pacific, the Union Pacific obtained control of a water route from New Orleans to New York by the Morgan line of steamships and shortly afterwards the Southern Pacific purchased a controlling interest in the Pacific Mail Steamship Company, which had a line of steamships from San Francisco to the Orient, opening up to Mr Harriman the possibilities of the Asiatic trade.

Continuing the policy which he had followed after obtaining the control of railroads, Mr Harriman began to rebuild the Southern Pacific. He proceeded on a scale that astonished railroad men and frightened financiers. His domineering personality brushed aside all opposition on the part of his associates, and that there was opposition was afterward acknowledged by the banker and philanthropist Mr Jacob H. Schiff. "Many times," he said, "we doubted the wisdom of spending so much money on the roads, but the result has more than justified the wisdom of Mr Harriman's policy."

The old grades over the Sierra Madre Mountains, near Reno, were so heavy that two locomotives were required to push short trains up the steep slopes at a cost which ate up a large part of the profits of the traffic. The only remedy was a tunnel seven miles long through the mountains, to cost from $12,000,000 to $15,000,000, and the tunnel was built. The Central Pacific lost 62 miles by skirting Salt Lake on the north over steep grades and sharp curves. Mr Harriman was told, as Mr Huntington had been told before him, that the mud in the lake was of a great depth. He drew a line from Ogden across the lake and the desert to Lucin and said to his engineers: "Build it. The decreased cost of operation will warrant the expense."

Twenty-three miles of trestle work had to be constructed across swampy flats and through water 30 feet deep in places, but the trains are running over the trestle today, and

Mr Harriman cut 44 miles out of 146 and eliminated 4,000 degrees of curves and 1,500 feet of grade. He spent more than $150,000,000 in rebuilding the Union Pacific and the Southern Pacific roads, but put the former on a 10 per cent and the latter on a 6 per cent basis.

This acquisition and rebuilding of a great railroad system was not accomplished without fighting, but if there was one dominant quality in the makeup of Mr Harriman it was courage. He never feared a battle, and he cared not who his antagonist might be. Wall Street and the world saw an illustration of this in 1901, when Mr Harriman, without hesitating for a moment, gave battle to J.P. Morgan.

For years, Mr Morgan's firm had directed the finances of the Northern Pacific railroad, and he entered into an agreement with James J. Hill, head of the Great Northern, whereby they would purchase the joint control of the Burlington. It was believed that this would strengthen the position of both roads. Mr Harriman heard of the plan and not only asked, but demanded a share. Both Mr Hill and Mr Morgan were more accustomed to making than granting demands, and Mr Harriman was refused. He started to get control of the Northern Pacific by buying the stock in the open market. For three days, a battle raged such as Wall Street had not seen for years. Millions were pitted against millions, and, as the price soared, thousands of speculators sold the stock short. Then each side, believing it had control, ceased to buy and called for the stock. Wall Street will long remember the panic that followed when it was found that Northern Pacific stock, thus unintentionally "cornered", went to 1,000 and the other stocks went down with a crash. It was on May 9 and 10 that the stock reached the high mark, and the financiers called a halt for fear of such a panic as would destroy all values. On May 11, there was a call for a meeting of financiers in Mr Harriman's office, and all the interests were represented. There was a compromise and Mr Harriman became a director in the Northern Pacific and the Burlington.

When the Northern Securities Company was organized, he put in his Northern Pacific stock, and when later the Supreme Court destroyed its existence he was offered a pro rata share of the stock owned by the company. This offer he rejected and demanded his Northern Pacific stock returned and won after a lawsuit. Mr Harriman continued in his ambition to control the railroads of the West, and would have gone much further if it had not been for the Sherman law, which prevented competing lines from coming under the same control. The Atchison & Santa Fe had maintained its independence. Mr Harriman became the largest individual holder of Atchison, and if that did not give him control of the road it prevented any other interest from obtaining it.

Mr Harriman made no secret of his ambition when he was a witness before the Interstate Commerce Commission, and he said that if they would let him he would go on and take the Santa Fe at once. "After you got through with the Santa Fe would you go on and take the Great Northern and Northern Pacific?" he was asked. "If you would let me, I would go on as long as I lived."

James R. Keene, the most resourceful freelance fighter Wall Street has ever known, crossed swords with Mr Harriman when the latter was winning his way to the top of the railroad world. Mr Keene had organized a pool for the purchase of Southern Pacific stock, expecting that a dividend would be declared. Mr Harriman decided to take his own time about the dividend, and Mr Keene brought suit, setting up that the profits of the Southern Pacific had been diverted to Union Pacific. Mr Harriman won that fight all along the line, and Mr Keene's friends lost money.

Wall Street has never had a dominating figure so secretive in his methods as Mr Harriman. When Mr Morgan or Mr Hill are about to put through a large deal some inkling of it gets to the public, but the first intimation of Mr Harriman's plans is when he gets ready to announce them. This was illustrated at the time the 10 per cent dividend on Union Pacific and the 5 per cent dividend on Southern Pacific was declared. There had been a meeting of the executive committee on Thursday afternoon, August 17, 1906, but no information was given out at the close. There was a feeling of unrest, reflected in the early quotations from London the following morning, and men who had purchased the stock on the expectation that a dividend would be announced were discouraged.

After the opening of the stock exchange, it was discovered that a notice of the unexpectedly increased dividends was posted, and this was followed by a day of speculation that set a record for that year. Mr Harriman did not come to the office that day. He was on his yacht, far from communication with Wall Street, but no one believed he was entirely unconscious of the excitement he had caused.

Mr Harriman was a consistent Republican, and was at one time very near the Republican boss of New York State. It was the time Benjamin B. Odell Jr was in the heyday of his power, and the closest friendship existed between the men. Mr Harriman never took an active part in politics, but once, however, and that was when he went as a delegate to the national convention which nominated Theodore Roosevelt for President.

The extent of Mr Harriman's influence with Odell came out at the time of the insurance investigation, when James

Hazen Hyde testified that Mr Harriman had advised him to make a settlement with Mr Odell, who had lost money in the flotation of the United States Shipbuilding Company. This Mr Harriman denied, but when Thomas P. Ryan went on the stand he said that Mr Harriman, when his offer to purchase an interest in the Equitable Society was refused, threatened legislative action and political influence. Mr Harriman was recalled and admitted that he had told Mr Ryan he would take action against him. It was when he was asked if he had taken any steps to thwart Mr Ryan's plans, he snapped out the historic: "Not yet." "It has been charged," the inquisitor said to Mr Harriman at that time, "that through your relations with Governor Odell you have political influence. What have you to say to that?" "I should say that Mr Odell had his political influence through his relations with me."

When the United States began its prosecution of alleged violators of the antitrust law, Mr Harriman became convinced that he had been selected as a target, and did not hesitate to say so at various times. With that courage which always characterized his action, he did not hesitate to break a lance with President Roosevelt. In a letter to Sidney Webster, Mr Harriman said he was at the White House shortly before the election in 1904, and that at the urgent request of Mr Roosevelt he collected $250,000 for the New York campaign. This money was raised on the promise that Senator Depew would be appointed ambassador to France, and he charged that the President had violated this promise. He spoke of the coalition of "Ryan, Root and Roosevelt" against him.

The President came back with a denial of the statements set forth in the letter, and it was at this time he made reference to "the shorter and uglier word", and later in the controversy referred to Mr Harriman as "an undesirable citizen". At the same time, he made public letters which showed their former friendly relations and which were addressed, "My Dear Mr Harriman".

One of the most notable of Mr Harriman's financial achievements was in April 1908, when the Erie Railroad was unable to pay notes that had fallen due, and it was threatened with a receivership. Mr Harriman was a courtesy member of the Erie board, but the financial interests supposed to be inimical to him were in control, and had been unable to obtain $5,500,000. A meeting to discuss the situation was in session at the office of J.P. Morgan & Co, and a no more critical situation could have confronted a railroad property. Mr Harriman made the offer to advance the money, and it was accepted at once. It was a personal offer and naturally gave him a dominating position on the board of the road.

According to the last issue of the Directory of Directors, Mr Harriman was on the boards of the following corporations: Baltimore & Ohio Railroad; Brooklyn Heights Railroad Company; Brooklyn Rapid Transit Company; Central Pacific Railroad Company; Chicago & Alton Railroad Company; Colorado Fuel and Iron Company; Delaware & Hudson Company; Equitable Trust Company; Erie Railroad Company; Guaranty Trust Company; Illinois Central Railroad Company; Ilwaco Railway and Navigation Company; International Banking Corporation; Leavenworth, Kansas & Western Railroad Company; Louisiana Western Railroad Company; Mercantile Trust Company; Morgan's Louisiana & Texas Railroad and Steamship Company; Nassau Electric Railway Company; National City Bank; New York, Susquehanna & Western Railroad Company; Night and Day Bank; Orange County Road Construction Company; Oregon

& California Railroad Company; Oregon Railroad and Navigation Company; Oregon Short Line Railroad Company; the Pacific Coast Company; Pacific Mail Steamship Company; Pere Marquette Railroad Company; Portland & Asiatic Steamship Company; Railroad Securities; San Pedro, Los Angeles & Salt Lake Railroad Company; Southern Pacific Coast Railway; Southern Pacific Company; Southern Pacific Terminal Company; Texas & New Orleans Railroad Company; Union Pacific Company; Union Pacific Railroad Company; Wells, Fargo & Co.; Wells Fargo-Nevada National Bank; and the Western Union Telegraph Company.

The New York Times, September 10, 1909

HARRIMAN HAD SAID THAT he was going to retire on his sixtieth birthday, February 22, 1908. That time came and he announced himself altogether too busy straightening out the "mess", which, according to his idea, President Roosevelt and the public had made in their attempts to regulate the railroads.

Still, the tide seemed to be settling against him. There was the Government's suit and his elimination from the Alton. Responding to the obvious criticism under the Sherman Act of a common control of the Atchison and Union Pacific systems, Harriman and his associates sold their Atchison stock toward the close of 1907 and have since sold the $10,000,000 par value which the Union Pacific held in the Atchison. The echoes of the personal controversy with President Roosevelt over the Sidney Webster letter were still awakened now and again, for when the President had no better example of the "malefactors of great wealth" against whom he particularly orated, he chose Harriman.

But a little over a year ago there was a change. It seemed

that the old Harriman programme was being put under way again. The Erie Railroad was threatened with a receivership, and it was Harriman who came forward when the Morgans gave it up with $5,500,000 of cash necessary to save it.

This episode was one which brought out strikingly the determination and resourcefulness which were among the characteristics of the man, which accounted in no small measure for the success of the constructive plans the results of which stand as the monument to Harriman's genius as a railroad man. Harriman, long a director of the Erie Railroad, stepped in to save it from financial ruin when the road had been given up for lost. He had to face the task practically alone, so little was the confidence of most of his fellow Directors in the road's future with its finances in the condition in which they then stood.

Harriman personally borrowed the $5,500,000 needed to save the road. He paid off the road's notes, undertook to supply it with many millions more cash, saw to it that the improvement work which the road had under way was kept in a year of seeing the road's earnings restored and its credit greatly strengthened. His friends in 1908 shook their heads at his temerity, but before long, in describing what he had done for the Erie, they spoke of his courage and foresight instead of his "temerity".

Announcement came later that the Georgia Central was now Harriman's, giving him a direct outlet to the Atlantic Ocean and the first complete transcontinental system under a single control. Then came meetings with J.P. Morgan in which their differences were adjusted. The newspaper headlines tell the story of the last year and a half: "Harriman in New York Central Board. Directors Retire Who Date from Commodore's Day"; "Harriman Says: 'I'll Look After New York Central'"; "Harriman Enters Guaranty Trust. Buys Half

Mutual Trust Holding of the Stock. Defeating a Union Trust Plan"; "E.H. Harriman Stronger Than Ever - Mr Gould, Head of Missouri Pacific, Pays Sweeping Compliment to Contemporary"; "Harriman and Hill Declare a Truce. Ten Years' War Apparently Ended by Conference of Railroad Men in California"; "Harriman Declares $13,000,000 Job of Electrifying the Southern Pacific" - and there we have the record complete right down to July 15, 1909, two weeks after he had gone abroad to seek treatment from the specialists of Europe in the vain effort to prolong his life.

That suggests the other narrative that has been running alongside this narrative of big things; the story of the sturdy little man with the tireless brain and eyes that looked as easily through the schemes of other men as through the vista of coming years. The little man with an ambition bigger than any other American before him, who proposed to put himself in command of the transportation business of the entire American continent. For that was Harriman's real ambition - no less - and he was in a fair way of seeing it accomplished when his starved body said to the brain that had robbed it of the chance to give the ambition proper support: "I can go no further. This is the end."

Imagine a man pursuing such an ambition as this and accomplishing it little by little, fighting up against the tremendous odds that Harriman encountered in 1901 and in 1903-1905 and in 1907, and you have a sufficient explanation for all the peculiarities of his character.

That he should have been able to go to San Francisco when the great earthquake and fire had laid waste the city, and in a few hours, almost, bring order out of the chaos of the relief work, at the same time arranging for the expenditure of millions in the construction of new and better terminals for the Southern Pacific, is easy enough to understand in the light of the man's ambition and accomplishment. Nor does it seem strange that on his return from that trip all he wanted to talk about when an army of reporters met him at the Grand Central Station was the record-breaking time that his train had made across the continent. All the rest was a thing accomplished, which needed no discussion from him....

That Harriman should have worked with an intensity of energy that made him the most crotchety, snappish and sudden of men in everything he said and did out of play time was quite as natural. Yet he had a keen relish for a joke. One day, when the Sidney Webster incident was on, he ran across a newspaper man he knew well. Harriman approached from behind. The newspaper man felt a sudden tug at his sleeve and looked around: "Say," said the master of the Union Pacific, "if that fellow in Washington had my job and I had his job, I wonder if I would make as big a mess of his as he would of mine."

On another occasion, a reporter from a paper that had published the most scathing editorial attacks upon Harriman and his railroad financing was sent to ask who were the two greatest railroad men in the world. "I'm one of them," came as quick as a flash, "and the other, in his own estimation, is the editor of your newspaper."

As Harriman lived to see his great ambition almost in his grasp, so he saw the accomplishment of his play-time dreams, the creation of a wonderful estate in the Ramapo Mountains, where he might realize what Carnegie has declared it impossible to realize: that he really owned a mountain. How the $2,000,000 which went to prepare that estate for his homecoming and death belongs to another narrative than this one. It has, in fact, been generously written already.

Of course, Harriman had his intensely human side - when he wasn't working. It showed itself in his devotion to his family, his love of horses and of the beautiful in nature, and his endowment of the Boys' Club, a $230,000 structure in the heart of the lower east side, where good health and good citizenship are taught together. There was a boy in this club who was asked a couple of years ago what he thought of Harriman. He said: "He's a great man. He's President of a railroad and worth a couple of thousand, anyway. He comes in, sees Mr Taber (the Superintendent) and goes on right about his business. He's a quiet man, and never tells anyone about his business. He ain't what I would call a fine-looking man, but I bet he could put up a great fight. But he ain't stuck up over it. He comes down here and says to Willie Schmidt: 'Hello, Bill', and Willie says, 'Hello, Mr Harriman, how's yourself?'"

That was the estimate of Julius Frieg, now 14 years old, who lives at 146 East Seventh Street. There are a good many that have known Harriman who will say that Julius was a keen judge of human nature.

Mr Harriman's wife was Miss Mary Averell, of Rochester, NY, whose father, W.J. Averill, a banker, was largely interested in the Rome, Watertown & Ogdensburg Railroad, and had large means. Five children were born - three girls and two boys. The eldest daughter is the wife of Robert L. Gerry, son of Commodore Elbridge T. Gerry. The second is Mary and the third Carol. The eldest son, Walter Averell, is just out of college and is learning the railroad business. The youngest, Roland, is 14 years old.

Winnipeg Free Press, Canada, September 10, 1909

EDWARD HENRY HARRIMAN BEGAN his career as clerk in a broker's office on Wall Street. He showed no unusual ability and for many years gave no promise of his later brilliant development. Socially, he was well liked and those who knew him at that time described him as a sociable young man, always full of fun. He was noted, however, for a mind of his own. What he wanted he generally obtained, but his desires and ambitions were, at that time, at least, neither very sweeping nor particularly important.

For a number of years, the brokerage firm of E.H. Harriman Co did a thriving business on Wall Street, speculating with its own funds and executing commissions for the Vanderbilts and other wealthy clients. It was not until 1883 that E.H. Harriman came actively into the railroad field. At that time, he had become known as a capitalist, one of the few who had gathered together a great fortune in the 10 troubled years between 1870 and 1880. He was credited with having in his strongbox a fair list of stocks he had picked up at extremely low prices during the various panics. In 1884, he was elected a director on the Illinois Central railroad. He was at that time working in close friendship with Stuyvesant Fish, who was elected second-vice president in the same year. Mr Fish had been a member of the stock exchange from 1876 to 1879, and the two voting men went into the Illinois Central to work along together. In 1887, Mr Harriman became vice-president and Mr Fish was elected president. Mr Harriman was then about 40 years old.

Whether Mr Harriman entered the railroad held in accordance with an already matured plan of his or whether his accidental acquaintance with railroad matters suggested to him the enormous possibilities of acquiring the control of large railroad systems is not definitely known. At all events, Mr Harriman's entry into the directorate of the Illinois Central railroad marked the beginning of his career as a manipulator of railroad stocks and reorganizer of railroad systems which, in the course of 10 or 15 years, made him one of the greatest railroad kings ever known in the United States, and placed him in control of more than 54,000 miles of water transportation lines and of railroad lines of an estimated length of nearly 27,000 miles.

During the panic preceding the election of President William McKinley, a number of large western railroads had gone to smash, among them the Northern Pacific and the Union Pacific. The wreck of the latter was particularly bad and seemed perfectly hopeless. A Morgan syndicate made an attempt to rescue the road, but gave up the plan in sheer disgust. But Harriman never lost his confidence. He formed a mixed syndicate, backed by Kuhn, Loeb Co, of New York, and including two members of the Vanderbilt faction, two of the Goulds, two of the Boston crowd that had sunk millions in the old Union Pacific and several independent capitalists, among them Harriman.

The road was merely a line from Omaha to Ogden, about 1,800 miles long. The syndicate paid the government $53,000,000 in cash and $27,000,000 to settle with the holders of the old first mortgage bonds. The road was turned over to the syndicate at midnight on the last day of January 1898. The same syndicate purchased for $3,300,000 a block of coal company bonds and other railroad bonds and in the following month a group of branch lines, called the Kansas Pacific for $6,303,000. That was the last dollar ever subscribed by the creation of the great Harriman system. The members of the syndicate received back every cent they had invested within three years and all the subsequent purchases of railroads were made on the credit of the Union Pacific and the few other lines under its control.

Harriman soon became the controlling spirit of the Union Pacific and by stringent economy, cutting off all waste and improving the rail line, transformed the road into valuable property, paying steadily increasing dividends. He cleverly used the credit of this road for acquiring, without spending a single dollar, the control of one railroad after another.

15

ALBERT VON ROTHSCHILD (OCTOBER 29, 1844 – FEBRUARY 11, 1911)

THE IRISH TIMES, FEBRUARY 13, 1911

*A*Reuter's Vienna telegram states that Baron Albert de Rothschild, the head of the Vienna banking house, died early on Saturday morning from heart failure. The Baron's death, which was entirely unexpected, causes general regret in financial circles, where his business capacity was highly esteemed. He was usually at the head of the syndicates of Austrian bankers in charge of Government loans. He was also a prominent figure in artistic and sporting circles, and was a very proficient skater.

Baron Albert de Rothschild, head of the Vienna branch of this famous family, was born in 1844, and married in 1876 Baroness Bettina von Rothschild, who died in 1892. Of this marriage there were six sons, of whom the eldest, Baron George, was born in 1877. Baron Albert shared an unusual distinction with his brother Baron Nathaniel. They each held a patent from the Emperor Francis Joseph granting them admission to the outer circle of the Austrian Court. Many officials of plebeian origin are present at the great State functions, but only the virtue of an invitation and not as a matter of right; and they are always excluded from more intimate functions, which are restricted to nobles. The only exceptions to this rule ever made, so far as men are concerned, are in favour of the Barons Rothschild, and the privilege was regarded as of such an unusual character that it formed the subject of a special decree published in the Austrian Official Gazette.

Baron Albert de Rothschild, like other members of his family, was the recipient of blackmailing and other begging letters. Of these, the most remarkable was a letter which was handed by a servant in livery to a schoolmaster who was on his way to Schillersdorf, the late Baron's hunting seat. The bearer of the letter asked the schoolmaster to deliver it to the Baron personally. The schoolmaster agreed to do this, and was continuing on his way, when the letter suddenly exploded, severely injuring the bearer. The police attributed the attempt to the author of some blackmailing letters.

Baron Oskar Rothschild, who was the youngest son of Baron Albert, committed suicide, as the result, it was said, of his father's refusal to let him marry the daughter of a poor Christian schoolmaster in Vienna, with whom he had fallen in love. Baron Oskar's death was attributed by his family to neurasthenia. He was only 21 years of age at the time of his death.

Baron Albert was the son of Baron Anselm Salomon von Rothschild, and the grandson of Salomon von Rothschild. The last-named, who was born in 1774 and died in 1855, founded the Vienna house of S.M. von Rothschild in 1826.

16

JOHN WARNE GATES (MAY 18, 1855 – AUGUST 9, 1911)

THE NEW YORK TIMES, AUGUST 9, 1911

*P*aris, August 9. John W. Gates, the American financier, died early this morning in the arms of his wife and son. The end was peaceful and it seemed as though he was falling asleep. The usual restoratives failed in the last crisis. Drs Gros and Reeves were present at his bedside besides the members of the family.

His iron constitution and courageous resistance, backed by every resource of medical science, failed to save Mr Gates. He had battled for weeks heroically with a disease of the kidneys, and when it was believed that he was almost sure to recover, contracted pneumonia. Several times he was reported to be at the point of death, but with the aid of powerful stimulants rallied.

The pneumonic and kidney trouble had ameliorated somewhat on Monday, but early Tuesday morning there was a recurrence of the congestion of the kidneys, which was followed by a further attack Tuesday noon. On Tuesday night, Mr Gates suffered a general relapse and gradually sank until death intervened. His wife and his son, Charles

G. Gates, had been at the bedside almost constantly since Mr Gates's illness was pronounced serious.

John W. Gates at the height of his activities in the stock market was perhaps the most spectacular figure that this generation of Wall Street has seen. Constitutionally a bull, it was the flood-tide of prosperity which followed the Spanish war, with the consequent great speculative opportunities both in the security markets and in industry that brought him his greatest successes. No one was more adroit at suddenly changing a position taken in the stock market, but it was as a bull that he made market history in Wall Street, and it was coincidentally with the ebb of the tide of expansion which had its spectacular climax in the panic of 1907 that Gates withdrew from his Stock Exchange Partnerships and announced his withdrawal from Wall Street.

At the time of his death, he was on the Directorate of eight railroad and industrial corporations, but was a powerful voice in many more. Up to the very last, he enlisted all of his energies in the development of the several large enterprises with which he was most closely identified, and worked with a persistency and closeness of attention which went a long way toward proving the sincerity of his statement that he was "through with the market". In these later years, he had in fact merely gone back to the exercise of his acknowledged constructive genius, and was carving out in the oil industry of the Southwest very much the same policies of aggressive manufacturing expansion which had put him at the head of the wire trade a score of years before.

It was business in connection with the Texas Company, his $50,000,000 rival to the Standard Oil Company, which took him abroad this summer. When he went suddenly abroad after giving his testimony in the steel investigation before the Stanley Committee his mission was said primarily to be to close a deal with Sir Weetman Pearson for the refining at the Gates Texas plants of the products of the English company's Mexican oil fields.

John Warne Gates was born on a farm at Turner Junction, Illinois, in 1855. His birthplace is now West Chicago. He began to show his business ability while still in his teens, and made his first speculative venture in a partnership in a thrashing machine, which netted him capital enough to buy the wood rights in a section of local timber. It was during this period and while he was still 19 that he married his wife, Dellora R. Baker, of St Charles, Illinois. The money earned from his thrashing machine partnership enabled young Gates to start a small hardware store in his native town, which gave him his entry into the wire business, through which he became one of the steel barons, enriched by the great boom in the steel trade which followed the Spanish-American war.

Mr Gates was comparatively unknown in New York when he burst into the limelight of Wall Street at the beginning of the first setback of the steel boom in 1902. At that time, as President of the American Steel and Wire Company, he anticipated the slump in the steel trade by closing down 12 of his company's mills. About 6,000 men were thrown out of work, but this action, coming at a time when the speculative public was still loath to believe that any halt in the upward movement of the steel industry was possible, roused the markets to the realization of the over-expansion that had taken place and brought in a small panic, in which Gates and his market following were said to have cleaned up a small fortune.

In the few years which followed that recession and in into the great bull market of 1905-1906, Gates made his greatest reputation as a bull leader.

It was primarily as a merchant that John W. Gates laid the foundations of his first fortune, and it was again as a merchant after scarcely more than a decade as a sensational market speculator, that he closed his career. His venture as a hardware dealer at Turner Junction began with the cutting of the great cattle ranges of the Southwest, and he quickly saw that a fortune was to be made in wire fencing. He sold out his business and made an arrangement with Isaac Ellwood, who was the pioneer manufacturer of barbed wire. His deal with Ellwood took him to Texas, where at the age of 21, he had the exclusive rights to sell the new product in the greatest cattle country of the continent. It is related of his beginnings as a salesman that he made his first hit with the cattlemen by building a corral of barbed wire in the plaza of San Antonio, into which he turned 25 range steers. This practical exhibition of barbed wire's effectiveness in taming Texas cattle started a market which, in less than a month, produced more orders than the Ellwood plants could fill.

Mr Gates then decided that the money was in the manufacturing end of the business and went back to Illinois. His first wire plant was started with a capital of £8,000, which built two machines. The organized barbed wire makers started after young Gates's new enterprise for patent infringements, but while the suits, which were eventually defeated, were pending, Mr Gates moved his plant back and forth between Missouri and Illinois and avoided service. Even during the time while litigation was hanging over his head, Gates showed his genius for organization by increasing his capital to $120,000 under the title of J.W. Gates & Co, and making profits of $150,000 a year. He then bought out his partners, and, in 1880, organized the Southern Wire Company, with a capital of $50,000. Two years later, he had consolidated with William Edenborn, later a Director of the United States Steel Corporation, in forming a combination of wire manufacturers in the Braddock Wire Company. It built a $250,000 plant at Rankin, Pennsylvania, and this was the beginning of Mr Gates's entry into the financial field. His wire interests grew into the Consolidated Steel and Wire Company, which was organized in 1888 with a capital of £4,000,000. Mr Gates was the organizing genius of this enterprise, which made money from the start.

In 1895, he was able to invest nearly a million in the Illinois Steel Company, of which he became President, and, a few years later, received an enormous block of stock in the newly organized Federal Steel Company for his holdings in this concern. It was at about this time that Gates first made himself felt in the stock market.

He had organized the $24,000,000 American Steel and Wire Company of Illinois in 1897, and, at this time, saw the possibilities of a combination of the big steel interests of the country which later developed into the United States Steel Corporation. One of his first steps into the larger field of Wall Street was the organization of the American Steel and Wire Company of New Jersey with a capital of $90,000,000. This and the Federal Steel Company, with $100,000,000 capitalization, were in the field in time to profit by the great steel boom which followed the Spanish-American war.

It was a period of rapid expansion and combinations were the order of the day. The public, having seen the immense profits made in the lesser combinations, were eager to buy stocks. Plant owners received almost anything they asked for their properties, and the promoters made millions at a rate which the country had never seen before. Gates, in getting together the Federal Steel Company and the American Steel and Wire Company, closed deals

involving millions overnight and bought plants on telephone order. With Ellwood, his associate in the promotion,
he is credited with having gotten together the combination
which was to become the second largest subsidiary of the
United States Steel Corporation in little more than a week.

Of this period, Mr Gates had a good deal to tell before
the Congressional Investigating Committee last month incidental to his examination in connection with the United
States Steel Corporation. At the time his Consolidated Steel
and Wire Company was in the field, profits in woven wire
were 50 per cent. Two-fifths of the plants he bought for the
consolidation were shut down and dismantled. He testified
that the United States Steel Corporation paid $46,800,000
in its preferred stock and $7,000,000 in its common stock
for the $40,000,000 stock of the American Wire Company.

John W. Gates was not taken into the Directorate of the
United States Steel Corporation. He was opposed by J.P.
Morgan, it is said. Whether the story of Morgan's opposition
is true or not, there have not been lacking in the succeeding
years many evidences of Mr Gates's willingness to come to
issue with the banker. One of the first market fights in which
the bull leader showed his generalship as well as the extent
of his resources, came almost immediately after the flotation of the Steel Corporation. Gates had by this time
acquired a nationwide reputation as a market operator, but
older figures in the Street had not learned to take account of
his boldness. His successes had made money for a large
following, and with their help he went heavily into Louisville & Nashville, then dominated by the Belmont interests.
The stock rose from around par to 150, and the movement
was looked upon as purely speculative. The news to which
the Street awoke one morning that "the Gates crowd" had
control of Louisville & Nashville was received with genuine

astonishment. He visited J.P. Morgan's office, and announcement quickly followed that the banker had found a customer for Gates's controlling interest in Louisville & Nashville.

The later campaigns of the "Gates crowd " in Wall Street centred around the bull movement which began after a brief recession in the steel trade in 1903-04. Harris, Gates & Co, and later C.G. Gates & Co, in which the leader's son, Charles G. Gates, was the senior member, became perhaps the largest speculative house in the Street. The "House of the Twelve Partners", as C.G. Gates & Co came to be nicknamed in the Street, was credited with carrying as much as $125,000,000 of stocks on margin in big market movements. It was during this period that John W. Gates, in association with Grant B. Schley, E.J. Berwind, L.C. Hanna, Charles S. Guthrie, and a number of others, acquired 200,000 shares of the stock of the Tennessee Coal and Iron Company. The same interests owned control of the Republic Iron and Steel Company, and steps were taken for a merger of the two companies. It was reported at the time that it was John W. Gates's intention to gather in a number of the independent steel companies with these concerns as a nucleus and form a rival to the "Steel Trust". The history of the failure of the plans of the Gates syndicate in Tennessee Coal and Iron and the purchase of that company during the panic has been told from several points of view to the Stanley Congressional Committee now conducting an investigation of the United States Steel Corporation.

One of the last things John W. Gates did in this country before he started on his last trip abroad was to unbosom himself before the Special Committee of Inquiry of what he believed were truths of the deal by which the syndicate was relieved of its top heavy holdings. He was never an unwilling witness, but, although he seemed to enjoy the chance of his day in court, he would not answer some questions because he said they did not look fair to some of the men whom the committee could just as well call as witnesses. He impressed observers as striving to deal fairly by his financial confrères, the committee, and the public.

The Republic Iron and Steel Company remained in the hands of Mr Gates and his friends. Significantly, perhaps, it was this concern which a few weeks ago broke away from the solid ranks of the other producers and started price cutting in the somewhat restricted range of its products, a move which was in direct opposition to the stand-pat policy of the United States Steel Corporation. The Republic Iron and Steel Company it was, too, which was given the credit or blame for starting the price cutting which followed early in 1909 a long period of stiff resistance on the part of the Steel Corporation and the independents alike to the demands of the consumers for lower prices during the business recession which followed the panic.

Because of the well-known market feuds of John W. Gates and his supposedly equally well-known position in the market on the eve of the panic, the rumors which became current early in 1907 that the House of the Twelve Partners was to be dissolved were taken as an indication that his enemies had taken the Gates scalp at last. He had been one of the most hopeful of the bulls in the Winter of 1906-7, and when the heavy declines in the stock market occurred in the first months of the panic year, the Street was willing to believe that Gates had been financially crippled. When the announcement of the dissolution of the firm finally came, Charles G. Gates put out this statement, which did not tend to discredit the theory that the old bull leader had at last been a heavy loser. "Father and I will retire from active Wall Street business for a year or so and give more or less attention to our various outside interests."

During the height of the bull market of the winter, the Gateses, father and son, had leased the shooting rights on the French estate of the Marquis de Beauvoir, at Sandricourt. As soon as the firm's affairs permitted, John W. Gates and his son went to France, and they did not come home from abroad until the panic had burst in full force in the spring. Before he left for Europe, John W. Gates denied with his customary emphasis the stories that he had gone broke. Later developments have proved that he left the Street with at least a fairly large fortune, and it was not long after the dissolution of his Stock Exchange firm that the story came to be believed in Wall Street that Gates had turned to the bear side during the winter and that during the "silent panic" of March the banks were carrying for him millions of free cash.

During the four years which have elapsed, the properties with which John W. Gates was identified have grown phenomenally. The Texas Company, which was the outgrowth of a venture made only a decade ago in the oil fields then dominated by the Standard Oil Company, has grown from a $2,000,000 concern to one with a capital of $50,000,000. In the same period, the Republic Iron and Steel Company, which a half dozen years before was not considered worth including in the United States Steel Corporation then forming, has become one of the leading independent manufacturers of iron and steel. Port Arthur, Texas, which was a dream of a railroad promoter when Mr Gates first appeared in Wall Street, is now one of the leading ports of the Gulf, and John W. Gates has been its upbuilder. He was the dominant factor in practically all of the industries of the town, was its largest real estate owner and was, as well, the principal owner of the Kansas City Southern, the successor of the Kansas, Pittsburg & Gulf Railway, which was the first reason for Port Arthur's existence.

The Washington Post, August 9, 1911

MUCH OF THE ATTRACTIVENESS that invested the personality of Mr Gates lay in the inability to fit him in satisfactorily in the scheme of life. Men who are easily classified are promptly disposed of and soon forgotten. With Mr Gates, his bigness was so pronounced that the temptation to call him great was all but irresistible. He was a rough diamond yet not a boor. With inexhaustible vitality, befitting his brawn and girth, he found a congenial place in certain spheres from which the mere make-up of a capitalist would have debarred him, and these tendencies won for him the sobriquet of "Bet-you-a-Million" Gates. Whether or not he enjoyed the appellation may never be known.

Cumberland Evening Times, Maryland, August 9, 1911

AMONG THE RECENT DRAMATIC instances of John W. Gates' life was his attempt to avenge the murder of his brother, Gilbert W. Gates, nearly 30 years ago, after he had been slain in a wagon, travelling across the blue-grass prairies of north-east Missouri.

Young Gates, who was but 18 years old, had been engaged in freighting in Sedgwick county, Kansas. Tiring of the work, he started back to his Illinois home. He was accompanied by Alexander Jester, a veteran of the civil war, who travelled in a prairie schooner. Jester took along a buffalo calf, which he exhibited along the route from the buffalo country to north-east Missouri. Near Middle Grove,

Missouri, Gates was murdered as he slept in his wagon. Jester drove into Paris, Missouri, that night and left the next morning for Indiana.

Gates' parents, Mr and Mrs A.A. Gates, of Turner, Illinois, becoming uneasy, Gates senior started in search of their son. At Paris, the father learned his son was last seen with Jester at Middle Grove. Jester was traced by means of the buffalo calf to Richmond, Indiana. There it was found Jester had started for the Kansas plains again. He was followed to Valley Center, Kansas, where he was arrested for murdering Gates. Jester escaped from jail by knocking down one of the guards.

For 29 years, Jester was lost. In 1899, he was arrested at Shawnee, Kansas, through information furnished by his half-sister, Mrs Cornelia Street. She said Jester had illtreated her and she desired that he be tried for murdering Gates.

When John Gates heard of the arrest, he said he would spend his entire fortune if necessary to have Jester hanged. He employed W.S. Forrest, of Chicago, and former Lieutenant Governor Charles P. Johnson, of St Louis, as his chief counsel to prosecute the case and hired 20 detectives to investigate. They found 100 witnesses scattered throughout the United States who were brought to New London, Missouri, at Gates' expense to testify as to what they knew of the murder nearly 30 years before.

When Jester reached New London in 1899, he did not in the least resemble the man who sat in a cell in the Paris jail 29 years before. Then he looked the part of a border ruffian, but when he stepped off the train at New London, he looked like an old-style minister and played the part so well he enlisted much sympathy. Jester wore a black Prince Albert coat and patriarchal long white beard.

Volumes of testimony were introduced at the trial, which lasted several weeks, and although John W. Gates spent many thousands of dollars, Jester was acquitted. Jester died four years ago in Oklahoma.

The Baltimore Sun, August 10, 1911

THE DEATH OF JOHN W. GATES removes one of the most picturesque characters of modern America, one of the most interesting of the great captains of industry who made the latter days of the nineteenth and the dawn of the twentieth century famous. Gates was an intensely human man, abounding in good fellowship, enjoying to the full the wine of life, warm-hearted, open-handed, a Napoleon of strategy in the amassing of wealth, a prince royal in spending his money.

His success was due, in addition to natural genius for money-getting, to his unfailing optimism, his unbounded belief in the ability of the country to grow up to be anything anybody could imagine for it. He bet on the resources of the country and the enterprise of the people, and the combination won for him nearly every time. That his methods were too often those of the man who would win no matter who lost, the testimony heard in recent investigation has unquestionably proved. But with him, business was a great game, and the fun of winning was the main thing, not what he won. The ill he did was done because of his reckless love of the game rather than from a mere desire to amass millions by trampling upon the rights of others. The tender side of him is well told in a paragraph from the news of the day. A reporter who had just finished interviewing him in his office, said, when Mr Gates turned to his work: "Planning to organize a new Steel Trust?" "Better'n that, better'n that. Writing a letter to mother."

Rochester Republican, Indiana, August 10, 1911

ONE OF THE MOST SPECTACULAR careers of modern times has been that of John W. Gates, steel and wire magnate, trust organizer, self-made multimillionaire, and racetrack plunger, who astonished the world almost as much by the nonchalance with which he was able to lose a fortune as by the ease with which he had acquired it. Outside of Wall Street and other financial centers, Gates was best known as a "millionaire gambler".

ISIDOR STRAUS (FEBRUARY 6, 1845 – APRIL 15, 1912)

THE NEW YORK TIMES, APRIL 16, 1912

*I*sidor Straus, who, with Mrs Straus, was aboard the Titanic, was born in Rhenish Bavaria on February 6, 1845. His father's family came to this country in 1852 and settled at Talbotton, Georgia. Isidor obtained a common school education, which he supplemented with a classical course at Collinsworth Institute.

It was his ambition to enter West Point Military Academy, and probably he would have done so had not the war broken out just at the time that he had prepared himself for that institution. He was then 16 years old, and, with the war fever in the air, he volunteered for the Confederate Army. He assisted in the organization of a company of which his comrades had chosen him Lieutenant.

When he offered himself, however, he was informed that the Confederacy did not have the guns sufficient to arm its men, and wanted no boys, and the only thing left for him to do was to enter his father's store and take the place of a clerk who had joined the Southern Army. Here, he remained for two years, when an opportunity came to him to go to

England and remain in the employ of a company there until the close of the war.

His father had in the meanwhile moved to Columbus, Georgia, and was seriously thinking of moving to Philadelphia to start anew in business. His son favored New York instead, and, his advice prevailing, the family came to New York and the firm of L. Straus & Son was organized and began dealing in earthenware. The success of this venture led the firm to branch out into porcelains and chinaware, and as the other sons of Lazarus Straus reached the age at which they could enter business the firm name was changed. From that time, the firm of L. Straus & Sons grew in reputation until it was known not only in this country, but throughout the world.

In 1874, the firm took charge of the china and glassware department of R.H. Macy & Co. This house had been established by R.H. Macy in 1858 and was already well known in the commercial world. Mr Macy was living in 1874 and was devoting his personal attention to a business that had already acquired a considerable magnitude. His death occurred in 1877. The business continued to grow - the Messrs Straus devoting themselves solely to the china and glassware department until 1888, when they were induced to enter the firm, the partners then becoming C.B. Webster, Isidor Straus and Nathan Straus.

Under the new management, the various departments of the house were much enlarged, until the present business of the big department store was developed. Isidor Straus has been the office member of the firm since the partnership was formed, but while the details of the office constitute his immediate field, he has complete mastery of the business. Mr Straus is a member of the firm of Abraham & Straus in

Brooklyn, of which the late Abraham Abraham was for many years the head. Several years ago, Mr Straus, with his brothers, Nathan and Oscar, who control Macy's, took over the Brooklyn store. In connection with their department stores, the Straus brothers have employed several thousand employees, besides maintaining cut-glass factories in Germany, Switzerland and France. His brother, Oscar Straus, was for many years ambassador to Turkey, and while there acquired a reputation as a connoisseur in Oriental rugs and draperies. Oscar Straus has been active as a supporter of ex-President Theodore Roosevelt, of whose Cabinet he was a member in the Department of Commerce and Labor.

Mr Straus's interest in political affairs was not thoroughly aroused until Mr Grover Cleveland became a Presidential possibility. It was then that he began to take an active part in legislation relating to a sound currency and tariff reform. In 1893, when the condition of business was desperate and grave doubts were entertained as to the position of President Cleveland with reference to the expediency of convening Congress in extra session, Mr Straus was prevailed upon to visit the President, and, while it has never been disclosed what his services were on that occasion, it is a fact that the proclamation convening Congress was issued on the very day that Mr Straus visited the White House. The result of that extra session forms an important page in the history of the United States.

Mr Straus took an active part in the campaign which resulted in Mr Cleveland's second election. He was later mentioned for the office of Postmaster General, but made it understood that he had no desire to give up his business pursuits for the position. He was later elected a member of the Fifty-third Congress and was a member of the Ways and Means Committee.

In the field of philanthropy, Mr Straus has held a place of prominence. The Educational Alliance, the "People's Palace" of the congested tenement district of the east side, of which he is President, owes its present position as one of the great factors in the solution of the sociological problem to his tireless work.

Mr Straus is a director in many and a supporter of almost every philanthropic and charitable institution in New York, regardless of creed. He is a Director in several banking and financial institutions, among which may be mentioned the Hanover National Bank and the New York County National Bank, and he is Vice-President of the Birkbeck Saving and Loan Company. He is Vice-President of the Chamber of Commerce and Board of Trade, and Vice-President of the J. Hood Wright Memorial Hospital.

18

GEORGE WESTINGHOUSE JR, OCTOBER 6, 1846 - MARCH 12, 1914

THE NEW YORK TIMES, MARCH 13, 1914

*G*eorge Westinghouse was more than an American; he belonged to the world, and had been a conspicuous figure in it for nearly 50 years. He died comparatively young - only four months over 67 - but he was still a youth when his career began. The air-brake, with which his name will always be associated, was in successful use when he was only 22.

It is said of that invention that it has saved more lives than centuries of warfare have destroyed. It has made possible the development of railroad traffic as it is known today - the trains of great length, high speed, large capacity, and increasing frequency. For this contribution to the service of mankind, Westinghouse received great reward and world-wide recognition.

He made many other contributions to industrial progress. If any of these deserve mention more than another it is probably his work in introducing and developing the alternating current system for electric light and power. In the early days of the electrical industry, it was soon found that the direct, or continuous current, could not be transmitted economically and efficiently beyond a short distance from the generating stations.

Mr Westinghouse, always alert for new ideas and new methods, found that in Europe apparatus had been devised for utilizing the alternating current. By these devices, current generated at high pressures could be transmitted over long distances and lowered in pressure at any desired point. He bought the patents, undertook to improve and develop them, and labored, against much opposition, until the alternating system became universal.

His career was a happy illustration of what the physicist Professor John Tyndall called "the scientific use of the imagination". He had a wonderful faculty for transforming visions into acts. He became eminent as an engineer, as an inventor, and as a manufacturer. Fifty thousand employees and $200,000,000 of capital were needed in the many organizations which he founded in America and Europe. And he himself worked as hard as any of the men.

His genius was never shown in brighter light than when he took up some task which other men described as impossible. He must have heard frequently that the air-spring for motor vehicles was impossible. But he made it successful. The world told him that the geared turbine for driving ships' propellers, and especially his application of it, could never succeed. But he made it succeed, and just before his fatal illness, he learned that two new battleships and a repair ship for the United States Navy are to be fitted with these inventions. He seems to have been an unconquerable man.

19

ALBERT SPALDING (SEPTEMBER 2, 1850 – SEPTEMBER 9, 1915)

THE NEW YORK TIMES, SEPTEMBER 11, 1915

*S*an Diego, California, September 10. Funeral services for the late Albert Goodwill Spalding, who died suddenly at his home at Point Loma yesterday, will be held privately at his late residence tomorrow, as his widow does not wish for a public funeral. The remains will be cremated.

The death of Albert G. Spalding, head of the sporting goods house of AG Spalding & Brothers, and of the American Sports Publishing Company, announced in *The Times* of yesterday, came as a shock to the sport-loving public of New York, to whom he was intimately and, as a sportsman, lovingly known.

In a way, "Al" Spalding was the "Father of Baseball", as it is played professionally. Most of the good there is in it today is the result of his initiative, for he was unique in combining ability as a player with positive genius as a manager, executive ability of a high order, and sufficient magnetism to hold men together when disasters of all sorts threatened organized baseball in its earlier tribulations.

Spalding started to get an education in a business

college in Rockford, Illinois. Incidentally, he played ball with a club known as the Forest Citys. His funds gave out, and his college course had to be abandoned, while he became a clerk at $5 a week in a retail store in the town. The men back at the Forest Citys' discovering his ability as a player, added to his income by employing him as a pitcher for their team, and fame came to him when he won for that club by his superior pitching a game against the National Club of Washington, one of the first Eastern clubs to undertake a Western tour to play what is now the national game, but then in the swaddling clothes of infancy.

His career, beginning with the Forest Citys in 1865, was one of continued success as a player. He was with that club until 1870, and it was his skill as an underhanded pitcher who could mix up the fast with the slow ones - for the ball was pitched instead of being thrown all through his playing career - that put Rockford on the map of the world. Henry Chadwick of Brooklyn heard of the youngster, went to Rockford to see him play, and on his recommendation Spalding became a member of the Boston Red Stockings in 1871. Among his associates were the famous Wright brothers, Harry and George, the former the Captain of the club. For the Bostons, Spalding won the championship of the United States and held it until 1875, when he went to the Chicago White Stockings, with the "Big Four" - Cal McVey, Ross Barnes, Deacon White, and himself - and helped win the pennant in 1876, thus winning the pennant as a pitcher five years in succession.

The following year, he became the manager of the club, playing with the team until 1878, and continued to direct its playing career until 1885, when he retired, giving place to James A. Hart and devoting most of his energies to the sporting goods business he had built up in the meantime.

It was while manager of the Chicago team, under W.A. Hulbert, its owner, that he helped to organize the National League, at a meeting held at what is now the Grand Central Hotel on Lower Broadway, in this city in 1870. This was made up of teams in the cities of New York, Boston, Philadelphia, Hartford, Chicago, St Louis, Louisville, and Cincinnati. It has stood the storms ever since and is still the major league of the country as he had dreamed it would ever be.

Discipline was almost unknown in most of the teams of those days and gambling on the results of the games an evil that Spalding saw must be eliminated if the game was to live. The supreme fight came in the year following the organization of the league, when it was suspected that certain Louisville players had sold out to the gamblers and lost games in return for cash received from the betting fraternity. Spalding took a brave stand, helped ferret out the wrongdoers and, backed by Mr Hulbert, had Bill Craver, Al Nichols, George Hall and Jim Devlin expelled from the Louisville club. This wiped out that evil which has never returned.

Mr Spalding was instrumental in taking the first team of baseball players to England, the Boston and Athletics of Philadelphia making the tour in 1874 and incidentally cleaning up the best cricket teams in England and Ireland at what the British players considered a ball game. It was he who in 1888 took two ball teams in a tour around the world and so introduced the game into the antipodes, where it has since become firmly established.

It was on this tour that Spalding was struck with the managerial capacity of John K. Tener of Pennsylvania, now President of the National League and at that time a pitcher with the Chicago club. Tener was treasurer for the party and managed the complicated finances and exchanges of foreign monies so well that Spalding prophetically but jocularly said to him one day, as they sat in the shade of the pyramids of Egypt, "Young man, you will be Governor of your own State some day."

While baseball was his particular hobby, Mr Spalding was actively interested in all sports. He was a stickler for absolute honesty and cleanliness in all of them. Though he had been a professional all of his active days, he was one of the most insistent among the lovers of amateur sports for pure amateurism, abhorred the pro-amateur, and did all he could to put a stop to the tainting of amateurism with the tricks which have occasionally brought it into disrepute. So strong and consistent was he in this stand that he was selected for the post of American Commissioner to the Olympic Games held in Paris in 1900, and every amateur commended the selection. His monument is a book entitled *America's National Game*, which is as near to a perfect history of baseball since its beginning as has ever been compiled.

FERDINAND VON ZEPPELIN (JULY 8, 1838 - MARCH 8, 1917)

THE TIMES OF INDIA, MARCH 10, 1917

*L*ondon, March 8. The death is announced of Count Zeppelin. Count Zeppelin died at Charlottenburg from inflammation of the lungs.

Ferdinand von Zeppelin was born on an island in the Lake of Constance in July 1838. He was the son of an official of the Court of Würtemberg. He entered upon a military career and had the good fortune, at the age of 25, to be chosen as the military attaché of Würtemberg with the Union forces in the American Civil War. While he was in America, it is said that he nearly lost both his liberty and his life as a consequence of his unconquerable love of adventure.

On his return to Germany, he found another war awaiting him, that of Prussia and Austria in 1866. He served through that campaign with distinction and also served through the Franco- Prussian War of 1870. In the course of his experiences in America, he had gone up in a balloon used for spying out the position of the Confederate troops. His enthusiasm was aroused by the experience, and the memory lay long in his mind. He retired from the army in

1891, 53 years old. He proceeded to equip himself with practical knowledge by means of apprenticeship in aeronautics, mechanics, electricity, sail-making, and meteorology. His aims and ambitions he described as follows:

"I intend to build a vessel which will be able to travel to places which cannot be approached - or only with great difficulty - by any other means of transport; to undiscovered coasts or interiors; in a straight line across land and water where ships are to be sought for; from one fleet station or army to another, carrying persons or despatches; for observations of the movements of hostile fleets or armies, not for active participation in the operations of actual warfare. My dirigible balloon must be able to travel several days without renewing provisions, gas or fuel. It must travel quickly enough to reach a certain goal in a given number of hours or days, and must possess sufficient rigidity and non inflammability to ascend, travel, and descend, under ordinary conditions."

He appealed, among others, to an American millionaire, the owner of newspapers, and was courteously told that "I never pay any attention to hare-brained appeals from visionaries."

From first to last, his work was enormously costly. His materials and the labour he had to employ were expensive on a scale far higher than that of inventors in other spheres. He sacrificed his own fortune to the work, and his family's, and still he was without success. In 1894, with little to show except his own enthusiasm and endurance, he appealed to the Prussian Government for a commission to investigate his work and prospects. It was refused.

In 1896, he obtained a sum of money from the German Society of Engineers, in Berlin, and was able to proceed with his experiments.

In 1900, on the second of July, some success was achieved. For the first time, Count Zeppelin actually rose from the earth in one of his own ships. He rose at 8.03pm, and returned at 8.21pm amid disaster. The ship failed to land without shock, and was destroyed.

The cost of repair was too great for the Count and the company. There was nothing to do but again to proceed with the work of appealing for funds, by personal canvass, by newspaper assistance where it could be obtained, and lectures or articles.

At last, in 1902, a measure of recognition was accorded him. He received a letter from the Kaiser. "Since your varied flights have been reported to me," the Kaiser wrote, "it is a great pleasure to me to express my acknowledgment of your patience and your labours, and the endurance with which you have pressed through manifold hindrances till success was near. The advantages of your system have given your ship the greatest attainable speed and dirigibility, and the important results you have obtained have produced an epoch-making step forward in the construction of airships and have laid down a valuable basis for future experiments."

In 1904, help came from the Government of his native state of Würtemberg. He was given the proceeds of a Government lottery and he again mortgaged such property as remained to him and obtained from these two sources about £30,000. This sufficed for the completion of his third ship. On October 9 and 10, 1906, he performed two successful flights. He flew 60 miles in two hours. This was taken to prove the possibility of steering and also preserving the rigidity of the ship during flight.

On June 20, 1908, his fourth ship went up. It rose at 8.26 in the morning, passed over Lucerne, Zug, Horgen Pass,

Zürich, Winterthur, Frauenfeld and Rorschach, and alighted in front of its dock at 8.26 in the evening.

On August 5, 1908, the Count rose in Zeppelin IV to fly southwards to Lake Constance to perform his 24 hours' test. He had almost completed it when, while he had left the steering for a few moments to superintend the repair of an engine, a storm arose, and the ship was destroyed.

It was then that the tide of fortune turned. All persons and classes came to the Count's assistance. Subscriptions were opened in every town, in every village, by every newspaper, and in organisations of all sorts. Rich and poor contributed together and the sum of £300,000 was handed to the Count within a few weeks. Since that date, the Zeppelin dockyard at Friedrichshafen, on Lake Constance, was established. "Today, it can turn out the airships of the largest size at the rate of one a month."

In 1909, Zeppelin II, the second of a new type, established finally the possibilities dormant in aircraft by a continuous 38-hour journey from Friedrichshafen to Saxony and back again to Würtemberg - a distance of roundly a thousand miles. A writer some years ago said: "Yet the Count has not reached the end of his aspirations. He still dreams of a wider and more wonderful field to conquer. He means, before he grows old, to explore in an airship the unknown country lying round the North Pole. With the support of the Government, and people, which he now enjoys to an unlimited extent, there is nothing to restrain him. For this next adventure, his preparations have already reached an advanced stage." But the war supervened and Count Zeppelin's invention was turned from possible polar exploration to the more ignoble purposes of destroying non-combatants and unfortified towns.

21

HENRY JOHN HEINZ (OCTOBER 11, 1844 – MAY 14, 1919)

THE NEW YORK TIMES, MAY 15, 1919

*P*ittsburgh, Pennsylvania, May 14. Henry J. Heinz, founder of the firm of pickle manufacturers that bears his name, known the world over for its sign of "57" and equally well known in church and Sunday school circles everywhere, died at his home in this city this afternoon after an illness of less than a week of double pneumonia. The firm of which Mr Heinz was at the head was about to celebrate its fiftieth anniversary in a few months.

Mr Heinz was born in this city on October 11, 1844, the son of John Henry and Anna Margaretha Schmidt Heinz, and after finishing in the public schools he attended Duff's Business College. Mr Heinz was 25 years old when he began in a small way the packing of food products at Sharpsburg, Pennsylvania, which was the beginning of an industry which he made famous the world over.

The possibilities of the industry dawned more vividly upon Mr Heinz at the end of three years, and so he removed his plant to Pittsburgh, where the business was carried on for some time under the partnership of Heinz, Noble & Co. The firm name later became P. & J. Heinz, and in 1888 H.J.

Heinz Company, which was continued as a partnership until 1903, when the business was organized as a corporation, with Mr Heinz as President.

Besides the main plant in Pittsburgh, with 22 acres of floor space, the corporation has 16 branch factories, 98 salting houses, 30,000 acres of land under cultivation, 40,000 people assist in harvesting the crops, 45 distributing centres, and prior to the war had more than 400 traveling salesmen scattered over America, Europe, Australia and Africa. The branch plants include one each in Canada, England and Spain, and the corporation has agencies in all parts of the world.

Mr Heinz was elected to succeed John Wanamaker as President of the Pennsylvania Sabbath School Association in 1908, which office he held until his death. He had been a member of the International Sabbath School Association since 1902, and last year at Buffalo was elected a Director. Since 1913, he had been Chairman of the Executive Committee of the World's Sabbath School Association, with a membership of 36,000,000, and this office practically put him in charge of that organization. Mr Heinz had planned to attend the annual meeting of the Executive Committee being held in New York this week.

Mr Heinz had been a Director of the Union National Bank, Western Insurance Company, Pittsburgh Chamber of Commerce, and was Chairman of the Commission to Devise Means to Protect Pittsburgh from Floods. He was also a Director of the Pittsburgh Tuberculosis Sanatorium, Western Pennsylvania Hospital. He was a member of the Aldine and Sphinx Clubs of New York, as well as the Japan Society of that city. He was one of the 50 members of the Inter-Racial Council, of which Coleman du Pont is the Chairman.

Surviving are three sons: Howard Heinz, now in the Balkan States representing Herbert Hoover's Food Commission; Clifford Heinz, at home; and Clarence Heinz, living in Wisconsin; and one daughter, Mrs John L. Given, of New York.

22

ANDREW CARNEGIE (NOVEMBER 25, 1835 – AUGUST 11, 1919)

THE MANCHESTER GUARDIAN, AUGUST 12, 1919

A Reuter telegram from Lenox, Massachusetts, states that Mr Andrew Carnegie died there yesterday. Mr Carnegie died of bronchial pneumonia after a brief illness of three days. He had been an invalid since 1917, following on an attack of influenza. Mr Carnegie leaves a wife and a daughter, Mrs Roswell Miller.

Andrew Carnegie was born at Dunfermline, in Scotland, on November 25, 1837, of humble parentage. His family went to the United States in 1848, and settled at Pittsburgh. The boy at first attended a small stationary engine, then became a telegraph messenger, and afterwards a telegraphic operator.

While clerk in the telegraphic service of the Pennsylvania Railway Company, Carnegie helped in the arrangement and adoption of the Woodruff sleeping car, then an innovation called for by the long distances traversed in America, and since followed up by the better-known Pullman and Wagner cars.

He was then made superintendent of the Pittsburgh division of the Pennsylvania Railway, perhaps the best of all the great American lines. As the Pittsburgh division included the big coal and iron districts round that large and smoky city, the appointment was an important one, and Carnegie filled it with success. He contrived to secure an interest in the oil wells then being boomed in Pennsylvania, which have since grown up into one of America's leading industries.

Then came the foundation of the concern with which Carnegie's name is always associated. He established a rolling-mill at Pittsburgh, which was the nucleus of the gigantic concern, known all over the globe, dealing with every branch and process in the manufacture of iron and steel. As one passes along the traffic-crowded lines of the Pennsylvania Railway into Pittsburgh, one is impressed by the sight of the big expanse of mills and sheds and the tall iron chimneys which mark the Carnegie works. To give some indication of the huge traffic in and about Pittsburgh, it may be said that normally over 2,000 loaded freight cars arrive and over 1,000 leave the city every day, and each of these carries three times as heavy load as do English goods trucks.

The Carnegie establishment, formerly known as Carnegie, Phipps, and Co, grew to be easily the first business establishment in Pittsburgh, and was only rivalled in its own line in the whole world by the big German establishment of Krupp at Essen. The firm was a great force on the side of high protection, and the tariffs made in the interest of the steel, rail and armour-plating industries were partly due to the political pressure brought to bear by the "lobby" at Washington, which was well supported by the Carnegie firm. Mr Carnegie himself was a prominent member of the Republican party and a liberal subscriber to the campaign funds.

By this political aid, the immense profits of the Carnegie business were built up. How large those profits have been was disclosed when a quarrel arose between Mr Carnegie and his partner, Mr Henry Frick - a quarrel which issued in legal proceedings. The Carnegie Steel Company was incorporated out of the two concerns of Carnegie Brothers and Co, and Carnegie, Phipps, and Co, each with a capital of $5,000,000, and the combined concern was capitalised nominally at $25,000,000. Within seven years, the annual profit was stated as $21,000,000 or 85 per cent of the nominal capital. According to Mr Frick, Carnegie estimated the net profits of the Company for 1900 at $40,000,000, and he himself at $42,500,000.

As a protected millionaire, Mr Carnegie was not too popular in America, and there was a good deal of trouble in his works, where the men employed were a cosmopolitan crowd representing nearly every nation in Europe. The troubles came to a head in 1893, when a veritable civil war on a small scale took place in that part of the works known as Homestead, situated by the lines of the Pennsylvania Railway.

Mr Carnegie was on this side of the ocean at the time and had nothing personally to do with the dispute. His manager, Mr Frick, a silent, determined man, was resolved to crush the union, and cabled over to Mr Carnegie his ultimatum, either to have an absolutely free hand or to resign. He was given the former, and soon Homestead was a scene of bloodshed. The State of Pennsylvania was first asked for troops, but the Governor did not see fit to interfere in what appeared to be an ordinary labour dispute. While the men erected a stockade round the works, Mr Frick secretly imported an army of Pinkerton "detectives" from Chicago, and a pitched battle ensued, many being killed and wounded. Women fought almost as desperately as the men. After the affair was over, the chief strikers were discharged. Mr Carnegie is said to have been exceedingly distressed by this tragic incident, for which he was held responsible. A year later, the Carnegie firm had another unpleasant experience. It was reported that there were serious defects in the armour-plating supplied to some of the American war vessels and an investigation took place which resulted in the discharge of a manager, but there was nothing to show that the firm itself was responsible for dishonest work.

The incidents alluded to were calculated to be the more damaging to Mr Carnegie since he had expressed strong opinions as to the evil of dying rich, and the duty of rich men to give on a grand scale to public objects. It must be said that Mr Carnegie carried out his own doctrines with sincerity and zeal. As long ago as 1879, he gave to his native town of Dunfermline swimming baths, and the next year a public library. In 1884, he gave $50,000 for a laboratory to Bellevue Hospital, New York. He has given about $2,000,000 to Pittsburgh and the adjoining city of Allegheny for a fine music-hall, art gallery, and library. He presented New York with the fine Carnegie Hall on Fifth Avenue, he also presented Edinburgh, Ayr and other Scottish towns with public libraries. He also gave or offered money to certain English political objects. He was interested in Irish Home Rule, and so offered a large sum in 1886 to the Liberal officials to forward that object. In 1896, he contributed to Mr Keir Hardie's election fund, but Mr Hardie would not take the money, but sent it over to the Homestead workmen.

One of the most notable and valuable of his gifts was the foundation of the Carnegie Trust for the Scottish universities, the main object of which was to open university education in Scotland to all who desired it but were too poor to secure it, by payment of the fees. The Trust has been ably administered by a committee consisting in the main of the authorities of the four universities. The democratic nature of Scottish university life made the step a simple one

in social aspects. The Carnegie student has taken his place among his more affluent fellows, and many of the most brilliant men turned out by the Scottish universities in this century have been sponsored by the Trust. An estimate of his total benefactions made in 1913 put them at over £40 million.

Desirous of spending some time each year in his native land, Mr Carnegie secured a Scottish estate in the Highlands, to which he added by purchase or rental, and there he has spent every summer for some years. He kept up the old Highland customs by having pipers playing at dinner, and in other ways, and thereby caused much adverse criticism in his adopted country.

At this place - Cluny - he received at different times many prominent men. Mr John Morley, Lord (James) Bryce, Sir Henry Fowler, and other prominent Liberals have been among his guests. On one of his coaching expeditions, the English poet Matthew Arnold was one of his visitors. Mr Carnegie generally spent his winter in New York, visiting, when occasion needed, his great Pittsburgh establishment.

He was in general demeanour an excellent compound of Scotsman and American, shrewd, acute, intelligent, never forgetful of the main chance, yet with the American hospitality and the Scottish regard for culture. Some of the charges brought against him as an employer of labour were not true. His men were well paid, and he did more for their mental culture than most employers.

23

JOHN DODGE (OCTOBER 25, 1864 – JANUARY 14, 1920)

THE NEW YORK TIMES, JANUARY 15, 1920

*J*ohn F. Dodge, the Detroit automobile manufacturer, who had been ill for a week with pneumonia in his apartments at the Ritz-Carlton, failed to survive the crisis of the attack and died last night at half past 10 o'clock. For some time before the end, he was unconscious and unable to recognize his wife and daughters, who were with him.

His brother, Horace E. Dodge, has been suffering at the same time with pneumonia, but he is now recovering and is expected to be out again within a fortnight.

The Dodge brothers, as they are known throughout the automobile world, have within recent years acquired a powerful place in the motor industry. Their chief product, the Dodge car, a machine of moderate price, proved popular almost as soon as it appeared on the market.

The Dodges were minority stockholders in the Ford Motor Company and in the autumn of 1916 they brought action against Henry Ford which led to a sensational trial. The plaintiffs sought to restrain Ford from using the profits of the concern to increase his production facilities, and they demanded that a sum, believed to be about $60,000,000, be distributed among the stockholders.

Circuit Court Judge George S. Hosmer decided in favor of the Dodges and ordered the company's profits treated as accumulated dividends and disbursed accordingly. He refused to allow Ford to build a contemplated blast furnace on the plea that it was a necessity for his plant.

John H. Dodge was born 54 years ago in Niles, Michigan, where his father was a machinist and iron worker, and it was in the father's shop that John and his brother, Horace, learned their trade as machinists, after they had attended the Niles school.

From their apprenticeship in their father's shop until the day when, by a coincidence, they both fell ill of pneumonia in New York, the two brothers were inseparable in work and play. It was in their early days that the two brothers demonstrated their enterprise by building the first bicycle ever seen in Niles. Graduating from the paternal shop, they began the life of journeymen machinists and worked in several Michigan cities. In Detroit in 1901, they laid the foundation for their great success when they established a machine shop. They started business with machinery they had taken in payment of a debt, and employed only 11 men.

As the business grew, the brothers divided the work. John Dodge became the business executive of the firm, while the brother developed as a gas engine expert.

About the time the Dodge brothers got their little machine shop to working, Henry Ford had completed his experiment in automobile building and was trying to organize a company to begin manufacture. In 1902, the Henry Ford Automobile Company had been organized and struck a bargain with John F. Dodge and his brother, by which they each were to take a $5,000 interest in the business, the stock to be paid for out of their profits in the manufacture of 650 chassis. That formed the beginning of the Dodge Brothers Company connection with Henry Ford.

24

JACOB HENRY SCHIFF (JANUARY 10, 1847 – SEPTEMBER 25, 1920)

BOSTON SUNDAY GLOBE, SEPTEMBER 26, 1920

*N*ew York, September 25. Jacob H. Schiff, widely known banker and philanthropist, died at his home here tonight. Mr Schiff's death was due to arteriosclerosis. He was stricken six months ago, members of the family said, but had not suffered to any extent until August, when he was compelled to return home from a sojourn in the White Mountains. His condition gradually became worse and he was confined to his home 10 days ago.

Mr Schiff's wife, his son, Mortimer L. Schiff, and his daughter, Mrs Felix Warburg, were called to his bedside this afternoon when physicians gave up hope of recovery. Two brothers, Philip and Ludwig Schiff, merchants, of Frankfurt-on-Main, Germany, also survive him.

The name of Jacob H. Schiff has been associated with the financial history of New York and of this country for more than a quarter of a century. In any list of the 20 richest men in New York, his name would find a place, his fortune being estimated to be at least $100,000,000. Likewise, in any reckoning of the country's most public-spirited and charitable citizens, his name would appear.

At intervals in the past 25 years or more, Mr Schiff took an active part in the financial development of some of the leading railroads and utility corporations in the United States. As head of the firm of Kuhn, Loeb & Co, backed by foreign capital, Mr Schiff supported the late E.H. Harriman in the great financial adventure by which the Union Pacific Railroad was reorganized in 1897, and in the subsequent transactions by which the Union Pacific obtained control of the Southern Pacific and other railroads.

This operation is regarded as one of the most important in which Mr Schiff engaged as a banker. It involved a vast sum of money, running into hundreds of millions, gave Mr Schiff a prestige among New York banking houses, which endured for the remainder of his life and contributed to make E.H. Harriman the best-known railroad organizer in the country.

Little less important was the enterprise which Mr Schiff undertook as head of his firm in placing in this country a large Japanese loan when Japan went to war with Russia. Some years later, Mr Schiff expressed regret that he had been instrumental in providing funds which helped to place Japan among the leading nations of the world as a military power. His remark caused a storm of comment in Japan.

Born at Frankfurt, Germany, January 10, 1847, Mr Schiff was educated in Germany and when 18 years old removed to New York, where he entered upon a business career, beginning as a bank clerk. A few years afterward, he became a member of a firm of bankers and brokers.

In 1875, Mr Schiff married Therese, daughter of Solomon Loeb, and became a member of the firm of Kuhn, Loeb & Co, of which his father-in-law was then senior partner. Mr Loeb retired 10 years later and Mr Schiff became head of the firm and continued as such to his death.

After his successful share in the financing of the Union Pacific reorganization, Mr Schiff became one of the most widely known and influential bankers of New York. He had been director of several of the leading banks, trust, life insurance, railroad and utility companies, including the Union Pacific Railroad and the Western Union Telegraph Company. His company acted as fiscal agents for some of the leading corporations of the country.

The name of Jacob H. Schiff stood for public service cheerfully rendered out of time as valuable as that of any man in the country. He was prominent in various forms of charity and philanthropy. He was vice-president of the Baron de Hirsch fund, founder and president of the Montefiore Home for Chronic Invalids, was one of the founders of Barnard College and contributed liberally to almost every Jewish movement or charitable institution and to many nonsectarian ones in New York. He gave generously to encourage the study of Jewish literature, gave $80,000 to found the Semitic Museum at Harvard, and provided funds for the establishment of the Jewish Theological Seminary in New York. Mr Schiff brought sound judgment to various municipal committees on which he acted. As vice-president of the Chamber of Commerce of New York and a member of its important committees, he labored for the commercial upbuilding of the city as zealously as for its political betterment. He was a director of the Metropolitan Opera Company, a member of the Metropolitan Museum of Art, the American Museum of Natural History, and the American Fine Arts Society. He gave a fund of $10,000 for the purchase of a Semitic library for the New York Public Library.

Mr Schiff was a firm believer in immigration and on many occasions expressed the opinion that the United

States needed more Jews. He did not approve of their remaining in the coast cities and felt that immigrants coming here should be sent to the inland States, where there was plenty of opportunity for them. He did not approve of the "money test" for immigrants on the ground that it would bar many honest and durable immigrants.

In 1905, a deadly bomb was sent to his office, but he was not in New York at the time. Clerks turned it over to the police. A similar bomb sent to another banking house exploded, but caused only slight damage.

Mr Schiff had a magnificent home on Fifth Avenue, New York, and a country home at Sea Bright, New Jersey. He leaves one son, Mortimer L. Schiff, a member of the firm of which his father was head, and one daughter, Mrs Felix Warburg, wife of another member of the firm.

JOHN DUNLOP (FEBRUARY 5, 1840 – OCTOBER 23, 1921)

THE TIMES OF LONDON, OCTOBER 25, 1921

*W*e regret to announce that Mr John Boyd Dunlop, whose name is familiar as the inventor of the pneumatic tire, without which the modern bicycle and motor car would be all but impossible, died suddenly on Sunday night, at his residence, Leighton, Aylesbury Road, Dublin, aged 81. He had been in failing health for some years.

His invention of the air-filled flexible tire was made in 1888, the first example being the work of his own hands. In the idea, he had been anticipated by R.W. Thompson in 1845, but the fact that at that time there were no vehicles for which a tyre was really needed may explain why nothing came of Thompson's patent.

The case was different when Dunlop came on the scene, for, though the motor car was little more than in embryo, the bicycle with solid rubber tyres was an established and popular institution. Dunlop was not then himself a cyclist: indeed, his invention was made originally for the benefit of his young son, John, who had a tricycle. The result of his experiment, however, was so immediately successful that a second-rate cyclist won all four races at Queen's College, Belfast, in May 1889, and thus demonstrated that the pneumatic tire was not only comfortable, but speedy.

Aided by the late Mr Harvey du Cros, Mr R.J. Mecredy, and a few other Dublin friends, a company was formed in November 1889, for the exploitation of the tire, with £25,000 nominal capital. The capital of successive companies covered many millions of money. In its earliest forms, the pneumatic tire was liable to bursting, puncturing, and slipping, and an enormous amount of ingenuity was expended on overcoming these defects. It revolutionised cycling, on the road as well as the racing path, and successive improvements in construction led to it practically making modern motoring possible.

The pneumatic tire is often supposed to be an Irish invention, but in fact Mr Dunlop was a Scotsman by birth and education, for he was born at Dreghorn at Ayrshire, on February 5, 1840, and after attending Irvine Academy obtained his diploma as a veterinary surgeon in Edinburgh in 1859. He migrated to Belfast in 1867, where he became a highly successful veterinary surgeon.

After he had patented his invention, he established a rubber tire factory in Lincoln Place, Dublin. The residents of Merrion Square, the adjoining residential area, raised an outcry on account of the fumes from the factory, whereupon Mr Dunlop established works at Coventry, and the Lincoln Place premises were used as a distributing centre for Ireland. Mr Dunlop was often heard to deplore the fact that Irish people did not share in the benefits which an ever-increasing tire factory would have brought to them.

Personally, he took little part in the commercial developments of the Dunlop companies, and had ceased for many years to be connected with them. In 1895, he became chairman of a large drapery establishment in Dublin. He was interested also in the motor businesses of Andrew Petry & Co, Dublin, and D.H. McDowell & Co, Armagh, and was largely concerned in the Australian wool trade. He patented several other inventions, notably a carburettor, which enjoyed a short vogue, but during recent years had lived in retirement in Dublin, where, having learned eventually to ride a bicycle, he became president of the Irish Federation of Old-time Cyclists. Last June, he contributed an article, "How I invented the pneumatic tyre", to the 36th birthday number of *The Irish Cyclist and Motorcyclist.*

Early last year, Mr Dunlop started an action against the Dunlop Rubber Company to restrain them from issuing advertisements representing him "in absurd or unsuitable costumes or attires", or in caricatures "calculated to expose him to public ridicule or contempt by misrepresenting his appearance or costume". Mr Dunlop's case was that in about 1891 he presented the company's predecessors in title with a portrait bust of himself and his signature to be used as trademarks, but that the company had placed his features on "the body of a very tall man, dressed in an exaggeratedly foppish manner, wearing a tall white hat, white waistcoat and carrying a cane and eyeglass", none of which it was his custom to carry. The Irish courts granted him liberty to issue the writ and serve it on the company out of jurisdiction, and in December last the House of Lords declined to accede to an application by the company that this order should be rescinded. Subsequently, however, a friendly settlement of the dispute was reached.

Mr Dunlop married a Belfast lady, who survives him. He had two sons, one of whom died 18 months ago, and a daughter.

The Irish Times, October 25, 1921

TO SAY THAT MR DUNLOP was a benefactor to his generation but inadequately expresses the effect of the invention which he gave to the world. The pneumatic tyre completely revolutionised road traffic. It was responsible for the development of the bicycle as we know it, and later of the motor car, and, as a high authority recently claimed, of the aeroplane. The internal combustion engine for land, sea and air was the outcome of the motor car. Without the pneumatic tyre, high speed automobile vehicles would have been impossible, and the motor car could not have developed a type of engine which eventually became the engine of aeroplanes.

In the romantic page of history which will portray the rise and development of the pneumatic tyre and automobile vehicular transport, the name of Mr Dunlop must occupy an honourable place. That page has not yet been written. It was Mr Dunlop's hope that, notwithstanding his great age, he would himself have been able to supply it, but this was not to be.

The fact that it was in Ireland that the pneumatic tyre was invented has given this country a special interest in motor matters, and it was one of Mr Dunlop's greatest regrets that Ireland did not benefit to a still greater extent from the industrial impetus which his invention provided. The holding of the first of the Gordon-Bennett Automobile Races in Ireland was at once a tribute to the inventor of the pneumatic tyre and the country.

Few inventors have lived to see the full development of the idea which made them famous, but Mr Dunlop, was one of the few. He owed this good fortune partly to his long span of years, but chiefly to the speed with which the new age turns inventions to the uses of industry and the money market.

Mr Dunlop made the first pneumatic tyre for a child's amusement. Within a few years, it had revolutionised the sport and industry of cycling. Then - still as a direct result of his invention - the swift motor car became possible and inspired the internal combustion engine, which in its turn endowed man with the supremacy of the air. We may say, without straining fact, that the air defences of England during the war and the flight from London to Australia were made feasible by an afternoon's work in a back-garden in Belfast.

Mr Dunlop witnessed and, being a philosopher, pondered all this marvellous procession of human progress. It would have been a less remarkable thing if that other Scottish inventor, James Watt, had lived to see today's vast railway systems take shape, like the bottled genie, out of the steam of his mother's tea kettle. The quiet veterinary surgeon's invention marked, and will continue to mark, a new epoch in the history of mankind; it has affected every phase of modern transport. It has changed every aspect of war - and, perhaps, in the long run, will help to abolish war. It has altered men's habits and modes of life by rediscovering the countryside, extending the suburbs of cities and towns, and reviving the Roman art of road engineering.

Judged by the impress of his work on civilisation, Mr Dunlop was one of the world's great figures. He has influenced the plain citizen's life more than Napoleon ever influenced it. Yet the world is a curious place, and no honorific gratitude came the way of this epoch making man.

The Scotsman, October 27, 1921

TEN MONTHS AGO, the late Mr J.B. Dunlop spent the last public social evening he was to enjoy amongst his Scottish friends in the automobile industry. Though not on the official programme of the annual Exhibition dinner of the Motor Trade Association at Glasgow, the inventor of the pneumatic tyre - a dapper little man with keen grey eyes and a flowing beard - in spite of the burden of his 80 years, enjoyed himself in full measure, and lived over again in conversation with friends, both old and new, the heroic days of 1888, when he produced for the tricycle of his young son, John, the inflated rubber tubes which have so materially helped to revolutionise the world's system of locomotion.

There were two things Mr Dunlop was proud of - his abstention from the use of either intoxicating liquors or tobacco, and his invention of the pneumatic tyre; albeit, his pride in his invention was tempered by what he regarded as the poverty of his own financial reward as compared with the enormous wealth of the industry based on the product of his brain. The only fortune with which he had been favoured, he considered, was that of sufficiently long life to see the pneumatic tyre developed and used to the general advantage of the human race.

It was probably natural that although he enjoyed a comfortable competence, he should fail to appreciate at its true value the services of a host of other collaborators necessary to the transformation of his original and essentially amateur effort into its modern form; but, at least, it may be said of him that he did not allow his personal disappointment to becloud his declining years, or to jaundice his outlook on life. He was a cheerful octogenarian, with an acquired Irish garrulity, which failed to mask either his

Ayrshire tongue or his sterling Scottish character. By the way, Mr Dunlop's is another instance, common in the field of invention, of the amateur fairly outstripping the skilful, trained mechanic.

His death this week takes one's mind back to "boneshaker" days, to the high ordinary bicycle (5ft 2ins, or thereabout), which required much youthful agility and temerity to mount; to the solid and cushioned tyre safety, to drive either of which involved much physical strain. It is astonishing to read nowadays that the new tyre was received with derision, and that when it appeared on the race track in Belfast in 1889 cemented to the rims of a bicycle ridden by a second-rate sportsman named Willie Hume, it was ridiculed as "an Irish home-made article", a "cart-wheel" and "roly-poly pudding", on account of the contrast between its 2in tread and the knife-like edged solid tyres then in use.

But the prediction of its inventor was verified. The fastest man on the track was the man with the Dunlop tyres, for Hume won every event in the programme against the pick of the English and Irish cracks; and at the Surrey meeting, at the Oval, the following year, G.L. Morris and Arthur du Cros carried off all the honours.

The new tyre was not yet established, but, while few realised it, the revolution in road traction had begun. A company with nominal capital of £25,000 was floated. The public were evidently sceptical, for only £18,000 were subscribed. The promoters were soon justified. Within five years, a dividend of 200 per cent was declared, and the capital of successive companies has covered many millions of money. The first factory for the manufacture of the new tyre was set up in Dublin. Unfortunately for Ireland, it was established in a residential quarter of the city, and when objections were raised to the fumes from the factory it was in time transferred to Coventry.

It is interesting to recall that when the pneumatic was brought out Mr William Erskine Bartlett, managing director of the North British Rubber Company, Castle Mills, Edinburgh, was experimenting with the cushion tyre, and within 18 months of the Dunlop discovery he patented the clincher, which was the first detachable pneumatic tyre. The Dunlop-Welch patent followed.

Personally, Mr Dunlop took little part in the commercial activities of the Dunlop companies, and had ceased for many years to be connected with them. Singularly enough, he was not himself a cyclist when, at the age of 48, he made his discovery. In his later years, he learned to ride a bicycle, and realised for himself the enjoyment he had been the means of bringing to millions of his fellow men and women. Scotsmen may well honour his memory, for he has laid the world under a debt of gratitude; as well as that of Thompson, the Edinburgh inventor, who as early as 1845 patented a pneumatic tyre, nearly 50 years too soon for the country to appreciate its valuable qualities.

26

THOMAS SUTHERLAND (AUGUST 16, 1834 - JANUARY 1, 1922)

THE TIMES OF INDIA, JANUARY 3, 1922

*L*ondon, January 2. The death is announced of Sir Thomas Sutherland. With the passing of Sir Thomas Sutherland, the Peninsular and Oriental Steam Navigation Company loses one of its figure heads, for though he retired from active participation in the affairs of the company as many as seven years ago, his service in the early years of its establishment and when it was in difficulties, and the way in which he directed its growth into one of the leading steamship companies of the world, has undoubtedly gained that distinction for him. As he himself remarked on one occasion, "So far as I am concerned, there is very little to say. The P&O Company has been my life, and all other things outside have been a mere fraction of my life."

Sir Thomas was born in August 1834 in Aberdeen. At 18 years of age, equipped with a sound education, he arrived in London, but did not find it a Golconda. His great career commenced with a junior clerkship in the offices of the P&O Company. The company, if it may be dated from the first attempt of its founders to open regular communication with the East, was only 15 years old when Thomas Sutherland entered its service. Its fleet was not very large, nor was its capital enormous, though, even in those early days, the Company was conspicuous for its possessions in ships. Sutherland's force of character, high intelligence, and grasp of affairs were soon made manifest to his superiors. His promotion was rapid. In two years after his entry into the company's service, he was appointed to Bombay. Thence, as chief clerk, he was sent to Hong Kong.

In a very brief time after his instalment in our Chinese colony, then a very young child of the Empire, the young Scotchman was appointed superintendent of the company's business in both China and Japan. He was only 26 years of age then. He would not say it himself, perhaps, but those who knew him then, have said that during the 12 years or more he spent in Hong Kong he more than doubled the company's business in the Far East, and established an almost impregnable position. He became a leader of men amongst the European community of Hong Kong, and took the chief part in the establishment of two great institutions, to whose existence the Anglo-Chinese settlement owes a great deal of its rapid growth in prosperity. These were the Hong Kong and Whampoa Dock Company and the Hong Kong and Shanghai Bank.

Both as a tribute to his great ability and useful public influence, Sir Hercules Robinson invited him to become a member of the Legislative Council, a singular honour for a young man of 31 years of age. But Mr Sutherland was managing director of the company in his thirty-ninth year, and chairman at 46. It is not often given to the most brilliant of men to reach the top rung of their ladder so early in life. Sir Thomas Sutherland in due time received honours from the Crown, in recognition of his many signal services, and from 1884-1900 was a Member of Parliament representing Greenock.

Besides being Chairman of the P&O Company for a period of 33 years, he was also Vice-President of the Suez Canal Company, Director of the London City and Midland Bank, and Chairman of the Marine and General Assurance Society. Among the honours conferred upon him might be mentioned the G.C.M.G. (Knight Grand Cross of the Order of St Michael and St George), and the degree of LL.D. (Doctorate in Law), while he was also a Knight of St John of Jerusalem and of the Legion of Honour.

27

ALFRED HARMSWORTH, 1ST VISCOUNT NORTHCLIFFE (JULY 15, 1865 - AUGUST 14, 1922)

THE MANCHESTER GUARDIAN, AUGUST 15, 1922

*A*lfred Harmsworth, 1st Viscount Northcliffe of St Peter in the county of Kent, was born on July 15, 1865, at Chapelizod, in County Dublin, Ireland. His father was a barrister with rooms in the Middle Temple and a considerable practice, being standing counsel for the Great Northern Railway. Thus, Lord Northcliffe was Irish in parentage and English in domicile, and the combination was apparent throughout his career.

Young Alfred Harmsworth was educated at a small suburban school, where also Mr H.G. Wells and Mr A.A. Milne began their schooling. The only remarkable fact about his schooling was that he induced his schoolmaster to allow him to publish a school magazine, of which he became both editor and manager. Thus, early did the trend of his talent display itself. At the early age of 17, he was taken into his father's rooms and became a student in the Middle Temple. But the law had no attraction for young Harmsworth. He longed for a more adventurous career. He found this in journalism, and the respectable student of law became a penniless Irish reporter. So poor was he during this period of his life that he had to share a room with a friend and had to earn his living by "penny-a-lining".

His first useful experience was when he took service under Sir William Ingram, helping him to produce a journal entitled *Youth*. But Alfred Harmsworth was one of those men who could not long be content to serve another. He found himself in journalism at a moment when the new reading public, created by nearly 20 years of Board schools, was longing for something less stiff and starchy than the daily papers of that period. George Newnes, with his weekly magazine *Tit-Bits*, had been the first pioneer in this uncharted region. Harmsworth determined to follow him.

So in 1888, he founded *Answers to Correspondents*, beginning with a one-roomed office in Paternoster Square. For a time, the paper went poorly. But within a year, Harmsworth had worked it up to a circulation of 78,000 a week. Then an idea occurred to him which, though it sounds absurd in retrospect, showed an instinctive capacity to grasp the interests and cravings of the average man. Harmsworth offered a pound a week for life to any man or woman who could guess the amount of the Bank of England's return for a given week. The effect on the circulation of *Answers* was prodigious. The office was inundated with postcards, and the sale of the paper went up from 78,000 to 200,000 in six weeks. The prize was won by a sapper in the Royal Engineers, who immediately married his sweetheart and "lived happily ever afterwards".

This device was only the first of an immense variety of ingenious schemes for gaining the affections and drawing the money of the public. As soon as *Answers* was fairly established, Harmsworth began to produce other journals - *Comic Cuts*, *Illustrated Chips* and many more. Amid this outpouring of inspired commonplace, he found room for all

sorts and conditions of men and women - *The Union Jack* for
boys, *The Sunday Companion* for the religious people, and
for women papers with such names as *Forget-Me-Not* and
Home Sweet Home. Within six years, Harmsworth had a
circulation order of nearly 2,000,000 a week, and was
paying out from £10,000 to £15,000 a year to his artists and
writers.

In the heyday of this sudden prosperity, Alfred
Harmsworth did not forget that he was the eldest of 11 children. He displayed that characteristic of family fidelity
which is so conspicuous in the Irish race. In 1889, he drew
his brother Harold (now Lord Rothermere) away from a
small clerkship in the Board of Trade to superintend the
business side of the Harmsworth house. In 1890, he called in
Cecil (since risen to high office), who had just left Dublin
University, where he had achieved brilliant honours in
modern literature, to look after the literary side of the business. A year later, he drew in another brother, Leicester, to
edit *Forget- Me-Not*. In 1893, he formed all these papers into a
company called Answers Ltd, with a capital of £275,000,
which afterwards became part of the Amalgamated
Press Ltd.

So far, Harmsworth's career had been typical of a kind
not uncommon in Fleet Street. He had displayed just that
knack of satisfying the tastes of the many millions of ordinary people inhabiting little houses in little streets which
has brought wealth to so many others in our time. But
Harmsworth's ambition went beyond that. He wished to
control and govern public opinion: in this endeavour he saw
both a fortune and a career.

He took the first step in this new development when, in
company with Mr Kennedy Jones, he bought the London
Evening News, in 1894, at a moment when that paper was in

very low water. It seemed a mad enterprise to attempt to save it. But Alfred Harmsworth and William Kennedy Jones made a strong combination. In his very candid book, *Fleet Street and Downing Street*, Mr Kennedy Jones has given us the frankest possible description of this early enterprise. The fascinating side of their work was the wonderful combination of daring and industry. There was no labour they shrank from, no task, however menial. Both men had been trained in the hardest school of journalism, and they superintended the production of their paper from top to bottom, leaving nothing to chance. The other side was an entire reversal of that old tradition of journalism which set up the journalist as a guide and captain of public opinion. This new school of Alfred Harmsworth's was frankly out to give the public what it wanted. Mr Kennedy Jones puts the matter in its naked brutality in narrating a conversation with Lord Morley of Blackburn. "You must remember," he said to Lord Morley, "that you left journalism a profession. We have made it a branch of commerce."

It was under such auspices and with such headlights that the *Evening News* was steered to success. The next step was the foundation of the *Daily Mail*, which started its famous career on May 4, 1896. The success of the *Daily Mail* was the climax of the second period of Harmsworth's life. The third was yet to be more brilliant. In the following years, the *Daily Mail* became the centre of a vast network of newspapers, all supplied from the same source and worked from a central machinery.

In 1905, those newspapers were amalgamated in a company called the Associated Press Ltd, with a capital of £1,600,000. Harmsworth was now a millionaire, and he began to receive the rewards conventionally allotted to great wealth by the governing powers of this country. Mr Arthur

Balfour, as a reward for his support in the Tariff Reform controversy, made him a baronet in 1904 and a peer in 1905. Mr David Lloyd George afterwards completed the work by making him a viscount in 1917. In due course, Northcliffe took a beautiful old Tudor House, Sutton Court, in Surrey, and there became a feudal magnate as well as a Fleet Street millionaire. In early days, he had married Miss Mary Milner, of Kidlington, Oxford. He has left no heir.

It was with all these achievements behind him that he was enabled to bring off the greatest stroke of his career when, in the year 1908, he purchased *The Times* newspaper. With the power of that mighty newspaper added to his others, Harmsworth was now able to wield a political influence never before possessed by a newspaper proprietor. On the outbreak of the Great War in 1914, he took a strong patriotic line. He threw the whole power of his newspapers into the conduct of the war. He urged with great insistence the appointment of Lord Kitchener as Secretary for War, but when Lord Kitchener displayed the limitations of his great intellect, Harmsworth subsequently attempted to destroy him. At the beginning of 1915, he acted as the instrument of Lord French in revealing the shortage of munitions on the western front, and the result was that Mr Asquith was forced to form the first Coalition government.

At the end of 1916, profoundly dissatisfied with Mr Herbert Asquith's conduct of the war, he helped to destroy the Asquith Coalition, and to substitute the Lloyd George combination. Under Mr Lloyd George's Administration, Harmsworth became chairman of the British War Mission to the United States, and travelled to America with that Mission. On his return, he became Director of Propaganda in Enemy Countries in 1918. But when, after the Armistice in November of that year, he claimed (as it was generally believed) to be a representative of Great Britain at the Peace Conference, Mr Lloyd George refused to give him that position.

The result was that Harmsworth, from that time forward, swung the whole of his press into hostility to the Lloyd George Administration, and during the following years carried on a bitter and persistent campaign with a view to its destruction.

Lord Northcliffe was the founder and the head of a new dynasty in British journalism; the innovator, or at least the exploiter, of methods, novel in this country although already acclimatised across the Atlantic, of conducting newspapers and influencing public opinion. The methods were phenomenally successful, whether viewed from the standpoint of popular vogue or of commercial gain. They made the reputation and the fortunes of Lord Northcliffe and of the Harmsworth family, of which he was the chief.

So far as the printed page was concerned, his genius lay in utilising and controlling the brains of others, and not in the exercise of any gifts of style or imagination he may have himself possessed. The quality to which he owed his rapid rise and his powerful influence was what has been described as intuitive perception of what the public wanted, or could be made to like, combined with bold decision in taking the shortest road to meet the demand. Though he often made mistakes, he had remarkable foresight in judging, or divining, what was the coming movement in politics and business or in social fads and whims, and in forestalling and catering for it.

28

GEORGE CADBURY (SEPTEMBER 19, 1839 - OCTOBER 24, 1922)

THE MANCHESTER GUARDIAN, OCTOBER 25, 1922

We regret to announce that Mr George Cadbury died yesterday at his home, the Manor House, Northfield, Birmingham.

George Cadbury was born on September 19, 1839, at Edgbaston, Birmingham. The family took its name from the village of Cadbury, Somersetshire, whence its members were scattered in various parts of England.

The founder of the Midland branch settled in Birmingham in the latter part of the 18th century and became a citizen of very considerable influence in the town.

George Cadbury was the second of the four sons of John Cadbury, who relinquished the ancestral tea and coffee business in Bull Street for the manufacture of cocoa and chocolate.

His wife was Candia Barrow, daughter of a Lancaster shipowner, and the family on both sides had for at least three generations belonged to the Society of Friends.

Although by the middle of the 19th century, the sharp division between the Quaker community and the outside world was being relaxed, the children of John Cadbury were brought up in the stern Puritan tradition, tempered by that liberal standard of material comfort which the prosperous Quaker families have consistently maintained. The boys were well educated, and while debarred from all amusements condemned as worldly, they were encouraged to ride and had no lack of outdoor recreation.

As early as 1849, John Cadbury had turned over the Bull Street business to his nephew and was giving virtually his whole attention to cocoa. Twelve years later, the management of the factory was entrusted to his two eldest sons, Richard being 25 and George 22; and the young men set to work to build up the gigantic concern which has now for more than a generation been famous throughout the world.

Together they applied themselves to their task without distraction or intermission. Year after year, from early morning until late at night, every working day they were at the factory, and they had their reward. Cadbury's cocoa began its conquest of the globe, and by the end of the seventies Cadbury Brothers found themselves brought up against the urgent demand for larger operations.

That was Mr George Cadbury's opportunity. Two decades of social and religious work, carried on in the Sabbath intervals of an unremitting business activity, had made him acquainted with the dismal conditions endured by the town worker, and the call for new premises found him prepared for a great social experiment. In 1879, he decided to remove the works, then employing about 500 people, from Birmingham into the country, and there to provide healthful surroundings not only for the work, but also for the leisure and domestic life of the firm's employees.

The undertaking was entered upon in the face of the ridicule of common-sense Birmingham and despite a good deal of misgiving in the Cadbury family. The plans were prepared with extreme care. An estate of about 500 acres was acquired; the Bournville works were built and 148 houses were put up, to be sold at cost price on leases of 999 years.

Mr Cadbury advanced the purchase money at 2 per cent, and himself planned the village, with a garden plot for every house, orchards, playing-fields, and a park of four acres secured from the house-builder, schools, clubs, and church. In a short time, the village of Bournville, the pioneer enterprise of a movement which has had worldwide results, consisted of 400 houses, 250 of which paid ground rent, while the remainder were let to weekly tenants. Mr Cadbury then handed over the whole property, valued at nearly a quarter of a million sterling, to the Charity Commissioners in trust for the nation. The control reposed in members of the Cadbury family during the present generation, but eventually the trust will consist of a body chosen from the Birmingham City Council and other local authorities and from the Society of Friends.

Although he resisted pressure from many sides (and from Mr William Gladstone himself) to enter Parliament, his influence in the political sphere was very wide. In later life, he entered decisively the field of newspaper proprietorship. He was already in control of several papers in the Birmingham district when, in 1901, the Liberal opposition to the South African War being most inadequately represented in the London press, Mr David Lloyd George and other leading Radicals induced him to acquire a considerable interest in the *Daily News*. This partial ownership did not work satisfactorily, and a few months later the paper became the personal property of Mr George Cadbury. From the first, Mr Cadbury had little to do with the actual direction, and very soon he left the paper entirely to others.

In private life, Mr Cadbury conformed in the most striking way to the popular notion of the wealthy and benevolent Quaker. He retained to the last the Quaker gravity of habit, in speech and dress and manner. He seemed to have no life apart from his business, his village, and his philanthropic schemes; and the family group of which he was the head was organised harmoniously as an agency for constant and arduous performance of good works. Mr Cadbury was twice married. His first wife was Miss Mary Tylor, and it was during her lifetime that, on the establishment of the Bournville factory, the family settled at Woodbrooke, now a social and educational settlement under the Society of Friends. On his second marriage, in 1888, to Miss Elizabeth Taylor, Mr Cadbury removed to Northfield Manor, the beautiful house which, with his holiday retreat among the Malvern Hills, was his home during the later years of his long life.

It formed, one would have said, a singularly luxurious background for the personality of the grave and simple old man, whose speech and bearing furnished no index to the power which had created the remarkable organisation of which he was the mainspring. There he dispensed a fine hospitality, especially to representative workers in public causes from every quarter of the world; there can be few houses in England which have received a stream of guests so variously inspired by religious and humanitarian ideals.

Mr Cadbury, needless to say, lived and moved in unquestioning acceptance of the evangelical faith, finding full satisfaction for the spiritual life in the austere ritual of the Society of Friends; but religious creeds and forms were no barrier or restriction in his eyes. The question of church or no church was for him a quite subordinate matter; he cared only for what a man was and what he did.

In carrying through the projects upon which his mind was set, he displayed an extraordinary tenacity and a disregard of opposition which was apt to be altogether disconcerting to his opponents. His influence was displayed in many unexpected places, and, as a matter of course, his help was sought by countless applicants, and many adventurers and busy bodies, not all of whom found him quite so easy a prey as they expected. To the end, though delegating much of the practical control of his enterprises to younger men, he retained the supervision of Bournville, riding or cycling every morning from his house to the works.

The habit of the early morning ride on horseback formed in youth was continued to old age, and the ways of Northfield Manor were in all essentials those of the Quaker households of Edgbaston a hundred years ago. After breakfast every morning, the family and guests gathered in one of the spacious rooms for worship. A hymn was sung, a passage of Scripture read by the patriarch, who then, if moved to prayer, offered the family supplication.

29

WILLIAM PAYNE WHITNEY (MARCH 20, 1876 – MAY 25, 1927)

THE NEW YORK TIMES, MAY 26, 1927

*P*ayne Whitney, prominent sportsman, one of the richest of Americans, son of the late William C. Whitney and brother of Harry Payne Whitney, died suddenly yesterday at 1.10pm near the tennis court of his country home, at Manhasset, Long Island, of acute indigestion. He was 51 years old.

According to Dr L.A. Van Kleeck of Manhasset, the Whitney family physician on Long Island, Mr Whitney had been in excellent health of late, except for occasional attacks of indigestion. Yesterday morning, he went to the indoor tennis court in the Whitney house and started playing tennis with Philip Boyer Jr, son of Mrs Philip Boyer, who was a house guest. Soon, he complained that he was not feeling well and retired to the lounge adjoining the court.

Mrs Boyer instructed the servants to call a physician and Dr Charles Neisley, of Manhasset, responded. He found Mr Whitney suffering severely from overexhaustion and his heart badly dilated. He administered a hypodermic, but within 25 minutes Mr Whitney died.

Mrs Whitney was attending a luncheon at the Colony

Club here. Word was telephoned to her of her husband's sudden illness and she started at once for Manhasset in her automobile. To make the best possible time, it was said later at the Long Island estate, she explained the circumstances to a motorcycle policeman, who then escorted her machine. She made the run from New York to Manhasset in slightly over 30 minutes, but Mr Whitney had died before she arrived.

At Mr Whitney's offices, at 14 Wall Street, it was said there was no information to be given out regarding Mr Whitney's death. At the Belmont race track as soon as the news was received, the flags were lowered to half-staff. The Whitney entries for the day were all scratched, including Whiskery, winner of the Kentucky Derby, and Valorous, both of which had been entered for the Withers Stakes. Mr Whitney was a director of the Westchester Racing Association, and while he had not an active racing stable, both his brother and his wife have been exceedingly active on the turf.

Payne Whitney was born in this city, the second son of William C. Whitney. Like his father and elder brother, he went to Yale, where he was graduated in 1898. While there, he achieved almost national fame as an oarsman and was captain of his college crew. After leaving Yale, he took a law course at Harvard, and in 1902 he married Miss Helen Hay, daughter of the late John Hay, Secretary of State and at one time Ambassador to Great Britain. He had met his bride through his room-mate at college, Adelbert Hay, her brother. The marriage, which took place in Washington, was a brilliant affair, attended by President and Mrs Roosevelt, but marred somewhat by the death a short time before of young (Adelbert) Hay. Among the wedding gifts was the house at 972 Fifth Avenue, which the Whitneys still have.

Mr Whitney took up active business after his marriage and was for many years a power in financial circles, although comparatively little was heard of him in that field. He was an active philanthropist in a generous but unostentatious way, so that almost nothing was known of his benefactions. The larger businesses with which he was prominently identified were the Great Northern Paper Company, the First National Bank of New York, the Whitney Realty Company, and the Northern Finance Company.

When William C. Whitney, died he left the bulk of his fortune to his eldest son, Harry Payne Whitney, about one-fifth going to Payne Whitney. The latter, however, inherited several millions from his uncle, Colonel Oliver Payne, a founder of the Standard Oil Company, who when he died was also a heavy stockholder in the Singer Sewing Machine Company and the American Tobacco Company. He left an estate of approximately $40,000,000.

An indication of the success Payne Whitney achieved in business is the fact that Wall Street estimates his wealth at more than $100,000,000, basing the estimate on the income tax payments that Mr Whitney made for the years 1924 and 1925. In 1924, he paid $2,041,951 in taxes, being in that year the third largest individual income taxpayer in the country, only Henry Ford and John D. Rockefeller Jr ranking above him. In the following year, he ranked fifth, paying $1,676,626, which amount was exceeded only by Mr Rockefeller, Mr Ford, Edsel Ford and Secretary of the Treasury Andrew W. Mellon. The Manhasset estate, where Mr Whitney died, was valued at approximately $3,000,000.

Personally, Mr Whitney was one of the most popular of men, genial and kindly, democratic, inclined to be retiring and always a thorough sportsman. He had been known, for instance, to glory in a victory for his wife's colors on the track, although the same race had cost him many thousands of dollars. Intensely interested in racing, he recently took to the idea of having his own racing stable, and not long since took up the breeding of thoroughbreds. He had been a great racegoer, and it is understood that yesterday before he began playing tennis he had arranged to go to Belmont Park in the afternoon.

Although he had been a member of the Jockey Club for many years, it was only recently that he consented to be elected to the Board of Stewards. From that time on, his influence was felt in the government of the turf. Though he had not raced nor even registered colors, and had only recently become interested in breeding horses, he had purchased, a little more than a year ago, the good English horse St Germaine from Lord Astor at a high price, and at the Newmarket sales last Fall he was the purchaser of several high-priced mares, paying in the neighborhood of $40,000 for Crispina, which is now in this country with St Germaine. A special meeting of the Jockey Club has been called for tomorrow at which resolutions will be passed and arrangements made for representation at the funeral.

Besides the Manhasset estate, from the name of which, Greentree, Mrs Whitney got the name of her racing stable, Mr Whitney owned the Greenwood Plantation in Thomasville, Georgia, and large acreage in Kentucky, where, last year, together with Joseph E. Widener, of Philadelphia, he added to his holdings by acquiring the old Colonel John T. Hughes estate. It was there that Mr Whitney and Mr Widener contemplated breeding thoroughbred horses.

In recent years, Mr Whitney took more and more time for sport and outdoor life. He was always active in aiding Mrs Whitney in the management of the Greentree Stables, and the liking of the two for sports has apparently descended to their son, for John Hay Whitney, generally known as Jack, is now in Spain playing polo. He is a student at Cambridge University, England.

There is also a daughter Joan, now Mrs Charles Shipman Payson, of Portland, Maine. Mrs Payson, it is understood, is living on Long Island, but word of her father's illness did not reach her in time for her to arrive at Manhasset before his death. Mr Whitney's sisters are Mrs Leonard K. Elmhirst, nee Dorothy Whitney, whose first husband was the late Willard Straight, and Mrs Almeric H. Paget.

It was not generally known that Mr Whitney, in a great many instances, aided his classmates at college to finish their courses. His gifts to the New York Hospital and to Bloomingdale Asylum have been many and large, and in 1923 he gave to the New York Public Library, of which he was a trustee for many years, $2,000,000.

Since the death of his uncle, he had continued many of the charities which his uncle helped support. Yale, his alma mater, loses a great benefactor in Mr Whitney, for he is known to have made many substantial gifts to the university, always, however, anonymously.

The funeral services will take place tomorrow morning at Christ Church, Manhasset. The Rev Dr Charles H. Ricker, rector of Christ Church, will officiate and interment will be in the little cemetery attached to the church. The funeral will be private.

30

SAM WARNER (AUGUST 10, 1887 – OCTOBER 5, 1927)

THE NEW YORK TIMES, OCTOBER 6, 1927

*L*os Angeles, October 5 - Sam L. Warner, Vice-President of Warner Brothers Pictures Inc, motion picture producers, died here early today. Death was caused by pneumonia, which followed an acute attack of sinus trouble.

Sam L. Warner was one of those who went into the motion picture business when it was really in its infancy, and with his three brothers, Harry M., Albert M. and Jack, built up the producing and distributing firm known as Warner Brothers. It was he who led his brothers into the film field.

Born in Baltimore, Maryland, August 10, 1887 [most sources cite Warner's birthplace as Krasnosielc, Poland], he showed a tendency toward the amusement business while still a boy. While yet in his teens, he obtained a position in an amusement park at Sandusky, Ohio. Motion pictures were just beginning to appear. Young Sam saw *The Great Train Robbery*, famous one-reeler of its day, and was inspired to seek a future for himself and his brothers in motion pictures.

He obtained a print of the film and a projection machine, and with his brother Albert toured the small towns of Ohio and Pennsylvania, thus conducting one of the early film road shows. They next rented a store in Newcastle, Pennsylvania, and turned it into a theatre. It had 99 chairs, rented by the day from a neighboring undertaker's parlor. When there was a funeral, the movie patrons had to stand.

That was in 1903. A short time later, all four brothers organized the Duquesne Amusement and Supply Company, and their business was booking films. After having experimented in the exhibition of pictures, they became pioneers in the exchange field and ultimately became producers.

The first notable screen success of the Warner Brothers was James W. Gerard's *My Four Years in Germany*, produced in cooperation with Mark M. Dintenfass. Other successful films followed and in 1925 the firm bought the old Vitagraph Company, one of the leaders in an earlier day.

In all these activities, Sam Warner was primarily interested in production and he recently became attracted to the idea of synchronizing pictures with sound. It was largely due to his persuasion, it is said, that Warner Brothers bought the Vitaphone last May. The Vitaphone Corporation was reorganized as a subsidiary to Warner Brothers and, as Vice-President, Sam took active charge of the making of the vocalized films. He was also a Vice-President of the parent firm, of which Harry M. Warner is the President.

Mr Warner married Lina Basquette, premiere danseuse of the Ziegfeld "Follies" on July 4, 1925.

31

DAVID BUICK (SEPTEMBER 17, 1854 – MARCH 5, 1929)

THE NEW YORK TIMES, MARCH 7, 1929

*D*etroit, Michigan, March 6 - David D. Buick, who spent a fortune on his dream of "horseless carriages" for all and reaped poverty in return, is dead today at the age of 74.

The emaciated, gray-haired manufacturer who lost out in the tumultuous industry he pioneered in, because of his inability to meet its financial expansion, died of cancer in Harper Hospital at 8 o'clock Monday night. He is survived by a widow and a son, Thomas Buick.

Until a month ago, Mr Buick had worked doggedly as an instructor in the Detroit School of Trades. Then, his waning strength forced him to remain at home. Two weeks ago, in the hope that an operation might help him, he consented to go to the hospital.

Mr Buick died as he had lived, uncomplaining against the fate that had tossed him into the discard while others carried on the business he started and made his name a power in the automotive world.

In order to make automobiles, David Buick in 1901 sold his plumbing fixture factory for $100,000. He spent it all and ran into debt before he developed a car that he drove from Detroit to Flint, Michigan, 68 miles, thus persuading President J.H. Whiting of the Flint Wagon Works to become his partner and backer. The new combination produced a series of half successes that served merely to increase its financial embarrassments, and finally the partners asked W.C. Durant of the Durant-Dort Carriage Company of Flint to take charge of the firm.

He consented, sold half a million dollars in stock to individuals in Detroit, and later organized the General Motors Corporation. The enormous difficulties that arose in the management of this huge enterprise caused Durant to relinquish its control to the du Ponts, John J. Raskob, Alfred P. Sloan and others.

Buick started an oil company in California, but again misfortune followed him in the form of ruinous litigation over land titles. Crossing the continent to Florida, he tried once more, in real estate this time, only to experience another defeat. Then he gave up, went back to Detroit, and since then had lived in such straits that he could not afford a telephone. And last Fall, the Buick Company celebrated the manufacture of the two millionth automobile bearing his name.

The Irish Times, March 7, 1929

DETROIT, WEDNESDAY. Mr David D. Buick has died here of cancer at the age of 74. He was a pioneer motor builder and founder of the Buick Automobile Company, now a unit of General Motors. He lost two fortunes, and his last years were spent in poverty. He lived here in a shabby little flat, and could not even afford a telephone, much less a car, though thousands bearing his name flashed past his door.

For the past two years, Mr Buick had been a teacher in a trades school. Mr Buick was a prosperous manufacturer of plumbing supplies when he began experimenting with motor cars, he impoverished himself before he was able to produce a practical vehicle.

32

ASA GRIGGS CANDLER (DECEMBER 30, 1851 – MARCH 12, 1929)

THE NEW YORK TIMES, MARCH 13, 1929

*A*tlanta, Georgia, March 12. - Asa Griggs Candler, founder of the Coca-Cola business, a philanthropist who had frequently aided Southern enterprises with his large fortune, died here today in Wesley Memorial Hospital, which he founded and in which he had been a patient since 1926.

His death had been expected two years ago after a paralytic stroke. He was 77 years old. The funeral services will be held on Thursday at the Candler home. Dr Franklin N. Parker, Dean of the Candler School of Theology at Emory University, will direct the services.

Mr Candler, starting with nothing, accumulated a fortune which was rated as one of the largest in the South. When he had amassed his fortune, he gave generously to worthy causes in the South and a number of times put his money to use in aid of his home city and State. He went to the rescue of the South generally in 1914, when the outbreak of the World War cut off the European market at a time when the cotton crop was ready.

Mr Candler was 10 years old when the Civil War began.

The family farm was near the path of desolation spread by Sherman's march through Georgia, and when the war had ended the farm was stripped of negroes, stock and provisions. He did his share of the work of reclaiming the land, at the same time attending public schools.

Later, he studied pharmacy, and when he was 21 went to Atlanta, Georgia, with a capital of $2.50. Going to work in a drug store, he remained until November 1873, when his father died and he returned to the family farm to take charge of it.

When conditions at the farm were such as to enable him to do so, he returned to Atlanta and in 1878 made his first start in business, forming a partnership with the late N.B. Hallman in the drug business. After four years, he purchased his partner's interest and conducted the business alone for six years.

In April 1888, Mr Candler first became connected with the manufacture of Coca-Cola and three years later became the sole owner of the business. Having confidence in its future, he staked his fortune in it and devoted all his time to it. His first factory was a small shed and he personally stirred the kettle in which the syrup was manufactured. The first year, the sales amounted to only 500 gallons.

Mr Candler organized the Coca-Cola Company of Georgia on February 22, 1892, and continued as its active head until 1911, when he was succeeded by his son, Charles Howard Candler. In September 1919, the business was sold to the Coca-Cola Company of Delaware for $25,000,000.

In addition to his gifts to charity, which aggregated several million dollars, Mr Candler's life was characterized by numerous instances of practical altruism, which in their inception appeared like tossing away money for the benefit of the public. During the money panic of 1907, he offered to purchase from businessmen property they wished to sell, not at panic prices but at the peak prices preceding that period. As a result he paid out $1,100,000 in cash for Atlanta real estate without demanding any sacrifice from the owners.

When the World War cut off the European cotton market and the price dropped to 6 cents a pound, Mr Candler went to the rescue of the Southern cotton growers, announcing his readiness to lend on cotton up to $30,000,000 on the basis of 6 cents a pound. After a large part of the amount had been distributed, he took off the limit and offered to lend as much as the South wished to borrow.

In 1915, Georgia found it necessary to refinance an old bond issue, one authorized by the carpetbagger government and which had been repudiated by the State during the reconstruction days after the Civil War. Mr Candler offered to take the entire issue, $3,850,000, at par.

At another time, Mr Candler was credited with having saved a rival bank, one of the largest in Atlanta, from liquidation by purchasing its entire capital stock and later selling it back to the former owners when conditions improved.

Mr Candler was elected Mayor of Atlanta for the term 1917-18 and during his administration loaned the city $360,000 to enlarge and improve the city water system. No municipal funds were available for the purpose and he advanced the money without waiting for the formal agreement by the city to repay it.

Mr Candler was a brother of the Methodist Bishop Warren A. Candler, and was one of the most prominent Methodist laymen in the South. His offer of an endowment of $1,000,000 was influential in causing the Methodists to select Atlanta for the new home of Emory University. His total gifts to the Methodist Church are said to exceed $7,000,000.

On January 9, 1923, he was the guest of honor at a dinner attended by 400 Atlantans, when two silver cups were presented to him, one for being the city's first citizen and the other, given by a local newspaper, for having rendered the greatest service to the city during the previous year.

Mr Candler was born on December 30, 1851, on a farm near Villa Rica, Georgia, the son of Samuel Charles and Martha Beall Candler. His father traced his ancestry to a William Candler of Callan Castle, Ireland. In 1878, the son married Lucy Howard, a daughter of his first Atlanta employer, who died in 1919. They had five children.

Mr Candler became engaged in 1922 to Onezima de Bouchelle of New Orleans, the former wife of Adolphe Rocquet. He broke the engagement, precipitating a $500,000 suit for breach of promise, which he won in February 1924. In June 1923, he married Mrs May Little Ragin, a widow, 35 years old, a public stenographer, whom he is said to have met first when she was working for an Atlanta law firm in connection with the De Bouchelle lawsuit.

The near relatives who survive are the widow, the five children of the first marriage, Charles, Howard, Asa Jr and Walter Candler and Mrs Henry Heinz; two step-children, the twin daughters of his second wife; and his brothers, Bishop Candler and Judge John S. Candler.

33

KARL BENZ (NOVEMBER 25, 1844 - APRIL 4, 1929)

THE SCOTSMAN, EDINBURGH, APRIL 5, 1929

*B*erlin, April 4. One of the pioneers in the construction of internal combustion motor engines has passed away in Dr Karl Benz, the founder of the famous Benz Motor Works.

Born in 1844, he was the son of an engine driver, from whom he inherited the taste for things mechanical. Very early in life, he devoted himself to the problem of inventing a mode of self- propulsion for street vehicles.

Whether or not he was the father of the motor car, a distinction claimed by various countries, he at any rate produced a two-stroke motor in 1878, and in 1885 a four-stroke tricar with 250 revolutions per minute and two-thirds of a h.p., which is now in the museum at Munich. An improved model soon after achieved a speed of 10 mph, and his exhibit at the Munich Exhibition in 1888 won the gold medal. His invention, nevertheless, found no support in Germany, and was left to be exploited in England and America.

When later the motor car began to become a marketable commodity, the firm of Benz at once took the lead in

Germany, where it has retained a prominent share in the development of the industry ever since. The capital of the firm rose rapidly to 8,000,000 marks, and in 1910 the output was 1,200 cars.

By the outbreak of the war, the capital had risen to 22,000,000 marks, but during the war the firm was turned on to manufacture aeroplane engines, submarine engines and similar military requirements. After the war, it soon resumed the manufacture of motor cars, and in 1926 was amalgamated with the Daimler motor firm, the combined capital standing at 50,000,000 marks.

It may thus be truly said that Dr Benz, who remained on the Board of Directors of the combined firms to the end, had lived through every stage of the development of the motor car, from its most primitive beginnings to its latest efflorescence.

34

SOLOMON JOEL (MAY 23, 1865 - MAY 22, 1931)

THE TIMES OF LONDON, MAY 23, 1931

*M*r Solomon Barnato Joel, always known as Sir "Solly" Joel, who died yesterday at Moulton Paddocks, Newmarket, at the age of 65, was a very prominent figure in the great diamond and gold industries of South Africa, though the greater part of his later life was spent in this country. He was also well known, both in England and in South Africa, as one of the leading owners on the Turf.

Joel Joel, the father of Solly and Woolf Joel, married Kate Barnato, the sister of Barney Barnato, and the two lads were practically adopted by their uncle. The Barnato brothers had already obtained a firm footing in the Kimberley diamond market, and first Woolf, then Solly, and finally another nephew, Jack Joel, joined the firm. When the Kimberley boom in claims and rough diamonds was suddenly deflated on the amalgamation of the diamond mines by Cecil Rhodes, the Barnato group joined the general exodus to the Rand. There, on the discovery of the famous Main Reef in 1887, a miners' camp of tents and huts had quickly sprung up where the city of Johannesburg now stands. Here the Barnato brothers, with Woolf and Solly Joel, built up a new and a greater fortune than ever the family had acquired at the diamond fields.

Solly Joel's own chance came after the boom of the nineties. Barney Barnato had become a Park Lane millionaire [before being lost overboard the passenger liner Scot in the Atlantic Ocean in uncertain circumstances in 1897], and Woolf Joel had been assassinated. The two deaths left him the active head of the firm, and by steady and skilful work over years, he consolidated two great enterprises - a vast expansion of the interests grouped into the Johannesburg Consolidated Investment Company, known as "Johnnies", and the virtual monopoly of marketing in Europe the output of the South African diamond mines through the Diamond Syndicate.

Actually, Barney Barnato had registered "Johnnies" in 1889. Originally, it had been his ambition to found a great bank. Gradually, that was dropped, and the Barnato interests were built up into what became - mainly under the guidance of Mr Solly Joel - the largest mining house in Europe. In connexion with "Johnnies", Mr Joel acquired, in 1910, the whole of the late Sir Joseph Robinson's interest in the Randfontein Estates, as well as Langlaagte, one of the great mines of the Rand. This purchase put the Joel brothers, Solly and Jack, into the first rank among the Rand mining houses.

Among Mr Solly Joel's numerous directorates were those of De Beers and New Jagersfontein diamond mines, in both of which Barnatos own vast holdings. He was also a director of the Premier Diamond Mine, the Standard Bank of South Africa, the South African Breweries, and the Four Per Cent Industrial Dwellings Company; and at one time he was interested in popular catering in London. Nothing gives a better idea of his skilful handling of a complex business than the mastery which the Diamond Syndicate has established in the world diamond market. Of this corporation, he was acknowledged as the ruling spirit, though the actual control was shared with the Union Government of South Africa and some others. Its object, obviously, has been to feed the market with just as many diamonds as can be absorbed, and its control has been on the whole to the general benefit.

Unlike most of the Rand magnates, Mr Joel took no active part in politics, and was never seen on a platform. His concentration on business brought its rich reward, and though he had the support of able associates, all important questions of policy were decided by him.

On the Turf, though, he never had the good fortune of his brother. Mr Joel won more than £340,000 in stake money. He first registered his colours in England in 1899, but he also raced on a large scale in South Africa, and was a steward of the Jockey Club in that country. His breeding stud at Maiden Erlegh was famous, but he did not depend on it alone for his racing stock, but paid a large sum whenever a racehorse took his fancy. Some of his purchases turned out wonderful bargains. For Polymelus, he paid £4,200, and won with him the Duke of York Stakes and the Cambridgeshire, and incidentally, it was reported, something like £100,000 in bets. The horse's progeny have won many thousands of pounds in stakes. Among other bargains were Bachelor's Button, Long Set, and Arranmore.

The nearest Mr Joel ever came to winning an English classic was in 1922, when Pondoland was beaten three lengths by St Louis in the Two Thousand Guineas. A misfortune recently overtook some of his horses in South Africa. A tornado struck his stables near Turffontein, and

Toureen and Janus, two valuable animals recently imported, had to be destroyed, while Glen Albyn and Oriental Knight were injured.

Apart from numerous private benefactions, Mr Joel gave the National Playing Fields Association 20 acres of land, which he liberally equipped, on the confines of Reading, near Maiden Erlegh. He had previously given an open space to Wokingham, and he and his brother, Mr Jack Joel, founded the Barnato-Joel Charity, endowing further with a gift of £20,000 a University Chair of Physics at Middlesex Hospital Medical School.

He married twice. After the death of his first wife in 1919, he married Mrs Benjuta, who, as Miss Phoebe Carlo, went out with a theatrical company to South Africa in the early days of the Rand. There are two sons and two daughters of the first marriage. Mr Joel entertained hospitably at Maiden Erlegh, and he also had Moulton Paddocks and a house in Great Stanhope street. He was very fond of the theatre, especially in its social aspect, and yachting and motoring were his other amusements.

35

WILLIAM WRIGLEY JR (SEPTEMBER 30, 1861 – JANUARY 26, 1932)

THE MANCHESTER GUARDIAN, 27 JAN 1932

*T*he death at Phoenix, Arizona, of Mr William Wrigley Jr, the chewing-gum manufacturer, is reported by the Central News. Born at Philadelphia in 1861, Mr Wrigley began business with his father in 1882, later removing to Chicago, where he started on his own account as a manufacturer of chewing-gum.

In 1911, the Zeno Manufacturing Company was absorbed by his company and the name of the corporation changed to the William Wrigley Jr. Company, of which he was president. He was also a director of the First National Bank, and the First Trust and Savings Bank, and was connected with various transport companies throughout the United States.

A keen sportsman, Mr Wrigley was president of the Angel City Baseball Club, and took a great interest in golf. He was a Republican in politics.

In 1930, when the depression in the United States led to a falling off in the demand for his speciality, particularly in the Southern States, Mr Wrigley carried through a huge deal, bartering chewing-gum for 100,000,000 pounds of cotton - a transaction involving a value of £2,400,000. In this way, he gave the impoverished American cotton-growers something to console them for the shortage of food.

His purchase of the island of Catalina, on the coast of California, as a holiday and winter abode was a great piece of luck. Experts discovered that it was rich in silver and lead ores, and he at once started operations to exploit them. He was a multimillionaire, and through his many directorships, an influential figure in American finance.

36

GEORGE EASTMAN (JULY 12, 1854 – MARCH 14, 1932)

THE TIMES OF INDIA, MARCH 16, 1932

*M*r George Eastman, inventor of the Kodak, has committed suicide by shooting himself.

George Eastman, who brought photography and its delights within the reach of almost everybody, was born in July 1854, a direct descendant of two pioneer families which settled in Massachusetts and Connecticut in the early 17th century. His father was principal of a commercial college in Rochester, but died when George was only eight, leaving the family in such a penurious state that his mother was compelled to take in boarders.

George himself began work in an insurance office at the age of 15. Later, he obtained a post as bookkeeper in the Rochester Savings Bank. He did not, however, let this humdrum daily work overwhelm him.

In his spare time, he attended what lectures he could and interested himself especially in science; and presently his scientific interest began to centre mainly round photography.

In those days, the taking as well as the making of photographs was a fastidious affair. The sensitive-coated glass plates had to be exposed in the camera while wet. In fact, the development, too, had to be completed before the emulsion dried. When pictures were taken out-of-doors, the photographer had to hang a complete coating and developing outfit with him, in a pack on his back, or in a wheelbarrow.

At first, George Eastman wished to simplify photography merely for his own convenience. Then the idea occurred to him that he might go into business on his own by making and marketing dry plates in the United States as another firm was already doing in England. Though discouraged by the uncle most able to help him, he purchased stocks of material and by June 1879 he was not only making plates which were "entirely successful", but he had also built an apparatus for coating them. That year he took out his first patent on account of the apparatus.

The next important problem in photography which Eastman set himself to solve was: "What could take the place of glass?" Photographers had been speculating upon a substitute for several years. Collodion had always fascinated Eastman. After long experiments with this material which involved work by night and day, he succeeded in inventing the first practical film in the history of photography. Needless to say, the invention was taken up everywhere. For the first time, Eastman found himself in a position to employ trained chemists to carry out researches for him. He manufactured his own printing paper. Then, in 1888, he began to make box cameras for his films - the first hand cameras in the history of photography.

Three years later, Eastman invented the daylight-loading cameras which proved immensely popular. *The Chicago Tribune* observed: "The craze is spreading fearfully... Chicago has had many fads whose careers have been brilliant but brief. But when amateur photography came, it came to stay." The Kodak slogan, "You press the button and we will do the rest", became the substance of as many jokes as the Ford was to become in later years.

In 1895, when the first pocket folding camera was made, Eastman began to take a deeper interest in selling his wares in foreign markets. It was some time before he was able to fulfil his ambition of "a house in Asia", but early in 1908 he concluded an agreement with Thomas Baker, of Baker & Rouse, Australia, by which the company obtained a majority interest in the business in the Antipodes, which made possible expansion in the Orient.

During the war, the Kodak business flourished more successfully than ever. It made enormous profits as a result of Government contracts, profits which later Eastman generously returned to the Government. This munificent generosity Eastman displayed again and again during the latter years of his life. He devoted the greater part of his fortune to the advancement of education, and had given by 1925 a total of over $58,000,000 for such purposes. Of this sum, the University of Rochester received over $25,000,000, including upward of $5,500,000 for the medical school and $6,500,000 for the foundation and endowment of the Eastman school of music. He gave also $15,500,000 to the Massachusetts institute of technology and about $2,000,000 to the Hampton and Tuskegee institutes.

By making photography available for everybody, and by lavishing donations on deserving causes, George Eastman made a major contribution to his age.

37

KING GILLETTE (JANUARY 5, 1855 – JULY 9, 1932)

THE NEW YORK TIMES, JULY 11, 1932

*L*os Angeles, July 10. King C. Gillette, safety-razor inventor and manufacturer, died tonight at his Calabasas ranch home, 25 miles northwest of here. He was 77 years old. Mr Gillette was operated on more than two years ago for an intestinal ailment and never fully recovered, his physician, Dr P.G. White, said in announcing his death.

Surviving are a widow, the former Alanta Ella Gaines, of Willoughby, Ohio, whom he married on July 2, 1890, and a son, King C. Gillette Jr. For the past 10 years, the family has resided in California, first at Santa Monica.

Years before his safety razor had been invented and the small packages containing tempered steel blades had become articles of household necessity the world over, King Camp Gillette envisioned a new and ultra-utopian social status.

In 1894, while he was a comparatively obscure businessman, Mr Gillette broke into print with *The Human Drift*, a volume in which he set forth his plans for his now celebrated "World Corporation", a billion-dollar organization

which would obliterate the evils of commercial strife, elimi-
nate crime and create a super-Socialist community. These
ideas, which called, among other matters, for a model
metropolis in the vicinity of Niagara Falls, were repeated in
two later volumes, *World Corporation* and *The People's
Corporation*.

To the world in general, however, Mr Gillette was known
for his razor and his razor blade. In 1903, the first year the
Gillette Safety Razor Company operated, only 51 razors and
14 dozen blades were sold. The next year 90,000 razors and
15,000,000 blades were sold. It is estimated that more than
20,000,000 razors and nearly a billion blades have been put
on the world market by his company each year since 1930.
Factories have been established in many parts of the world,
and the picture of Mr Gillette on the blade wrappers is
familiar to people all over the globe.

Mr Gillette was born at Fond du Lac, Wisconsin, on
January 5, 1855. His father, George Wolcott Gillette, was
somewhat of an inventor. His mother, the former Fanny
Lemira Camp, was the author of the *White House Cook Book*,
which still is in great demand.

When Mr Gillette was four years old, the family moved
to Chicago. His education was acquired in the public
schools. While still a youth, he was employed by a hardware
firm for two years. After similar work in New York City,
young Gillette went to Kansas City and worked as a traveling salesman for a hardware firm, later representing the
company in England. In 1889, he returned to this country
and worked for a bottle-stopper manufacturing company
for 10 years, part of which were spent in the United States
and part in England.

It was during the latter half of this term of service that
Mr Gillette perfected his safety razor. He returned to the

United States in 1904 and, with signal success, set about
organizing this new American industry. The younger generation took to the new idea with enthusiasm and many of the
older, tired of cutting themselves with old-fashioned razors,
changed their habits. A few years ago, the British Army,
hitherto equipped with ordinary razors, was equipped with
Gillette razors and blades.

Despite his great success in the industrial field, which he
practically monopolized for a few years, Mr Gillette was
very busy with his plans for a new social order. In *The
Human Drift*, he suggested a new type of city at the power
sources of Niagara Falls. He planned gigantic apartment
houses of modern hospital design. His world was described
as one where no gold was to be hoarded and there was to be
no want for material necessities or even luxuries. It would
be a world of united intelligence and material equality,
where crime would be unknown because commercial
competition was nonexistent.

The *World Corporation* was actually incorporated under
the laws of Arizona in 1910. At that time, its originator
predicted "horizonless farms, trafficless streets bordered
with grass and flowers", and many other innovations. Everything would be merged, and he offered the presidency of the
trust to President Theodore Roosevelt, who was again a
private citizen, for a period of four years at a stipend of
$1,000,000. Colonel Roosevelt declined.

Mr Gillette was a Republican, a thirty-two-degree Mason
and a member of the following clubs: California, Athletic,
Los Angeles Country, Hollywood Country, and Brentwood
Country.

38

FREDERICK HENRY ROYCE (MARCH 27, 1863 – APRIL 22, 1933)

THE MANCHESTER GUARDIAN, APRIL 24, 1933

*S*ir Frederick Henry Royce, the famous maker of motor-cars and aeroplane engines, whose death is announced on another page, came of country stock. He was the son of an Alwalton farmer, and was forced to earn his living at an early age as a newsboy to Messrs W.H. Smith & Son. But the energy and versatility of the boy and his strong leaning towards mechanical matters induced some of his father's friends to find him an apprenticeship with the Great Northern Railway Company, and for three years he worked with the company at Peterborough, studying in the evenings at the Technical College.

After he left the railway company, he worked in various capacities and places - as a telegraph boy in London, in a machine-tool factory at 11s a week, in an armament factory in Leeds, and with a firm manufacturing arc-lamps, in whose Liverpool branch he became chief electrical engineer. When this company went out of business, Mr Royce founded a similar company of his own, Messrs Royce Ltd, of Manchester, which at first made only lamps and dynamos, but which later extended its range and still produces electric cranes and motors.

In 1902, he turned his attention to the motor-car, whose early and unreliable examples were then appearing on the roads. He bought one for himself, and was so dissatisfied at its performance that in the following year he produced a model of his own, a two-cylinder, 10-hp car. Four years later, he met the Honourable C.S. Rolls, another pioneer of the internal-combustion engine and a keen aviator, and with him formed the famous firm of Rolls-Royce Ltd. The works were moved in 1908 to Derby, where they have remained ever since producing the cars which have become the standard of excellence and precision the world over.

On the outbreak of war, the need for reliable aeroplane engines became suddenly pressing, and the firm had to prepare for enormous production for the Government. Mr Royce turned this opportunity to good account, and the engines he designed soon gained the same reputation for general excellence that his motor-cars had won, and they are now used by a large number of the civil and military aircraft of the world.

The machines which won the Schneider Cup in 1929 and 1931 carried Rolls-Royce engines, and the world records set up by Sir Malcolm Campbell recently on land, and by Mr Kaye Don on the water, and the record made by Flight Lieutenant George Stainforth in the last Schneider Cup race of 407 miles per hour, which has been beaten in the last few days by an Italian airman, were all achieved on Rolls-Royce engines. Mr Royce also designed the engine used by Sir John Alcock and Sir Arthur Whitten Brown on their first Atlantic flight.

In 1930, the King conferred on him a baronetcy in

consideration of his services to the country. After his retirement to West Wittering, Sir Henry did not give up his work, but a staff of designers was continually with him in his home, and he kept in the closest touch with the Derby factory.

39

CHARLES FLINT (JANUARY 24, 1850 – FEBRUARY 13, 1934)

THE NEW YORK TIMES, FEBRUARY 14, 1934

ashington, February 13. Charles R. Flint died at his apartment at the Shoreham Hotel here last night at the age of 84. Mr Flint, who had been an invalid for two years, suffered a stroke on Saturday. He is survived by his widow, Mrs Charlotte Reeves Flint. A funeral service will be held Thursday in the Mount Pleasant Heights Presbyterian Church.

When he was 73 years old, Mr Flint decided it was time to record his experiences and he wrote *Memories of an Active Life - Men and Ships and Sealing Wax*. He was by no means through with active business, however, and he continued until 1931, when he was 81.

His memoirs revealed that he was an expert on sports, politics, trustmaking, high finance, filibustering and many other things. He wrote of his adventures in supporting tottering thrones; setting up or pulling down tropical republics; advocating Pan-Americanism; creating giant corporations; trout fishing; intrigues in China and intrigues at home.

The "father of trusts" had such an uneventful life that

such matters as organizing the Pacific Coast Clipper Line, between New York and San Francisco; selling warships to Japan and later to Russia; being chairman of the organization which consolidated the street railways at Syracuse, New York, and acting as a confidential agent to the United States Government were mere incidents.

His chief occupation, however, was the organization of trusts and corporations, some of which were among the best known and most powerful in this country.

He retired for the first time in 1928 at the age of 78, after the death of his first wife and his second marriage, declaring greed was the impelling force that made millionaires go on increasing their wealth after they had acquired millions, instead of retiring and enjoying life.

For two years thereafter, he passed his time principally in motoring through the country and in hunting and fishing, meditating on the "horizontal" combinations that he had launched, such as the American Woolen Company, the American Chicle Company, the Mechanical Rubber Company, New York Belting and Packing Company, International Business Machines Corporation, and a score of others.

In 1930, however, explaining that he no longer could bear inactivity, he returned to his old office at 25 Broad Street, and announced that he saw the possibility of further industrial organization in the form of "vertical" and "circular" combinations.

Mr Flint found, however, that his age was considered a bar to leadership in great new enterprises even though his prestige was welcome. He argued against this judgment for another year, and then decided to retire for the second and last time in 1931, at the age of 81.

The son of the owner of a fleet of clipper ships in Maine,

he came to New York in 1866 to make his own way. He made his business start with the shipping firm of W.R. Grace in downtown New York, working for two years without a cent of pay in order to learn the ropes. When he was 18, he formed a ship chandlery concern with two other young men under the name of Gilchrist, Flint & Co. A few years later, he sold his interest in the chandlery and went back to Grace as a partner in W.R. Grace & Co, receiving a 22 per cent interest in the Grace companies in New York, Chile, San Francisco and Peru.

He was a Grace partner for 13 years, leaving the concern eventually to found Flint & Co at 25 Broad Street, where he did business during the remainder of a career that took him to many interesting fields and brought him into contact with crowned heads and men of note throughout the world.

The firm of Flint & Co - shipowners, lumber and general merchandise - had been founded by his father, Benjamin Flint, in 1837. Mr Flint joined it in 1885.

From 1877 to 1879, he had been Consul in New York for Chile. He resigned that post when trouble arose between Chile and Peru, as he had important interests in the latter republic. Later, he was Consul General for Costa Rica and Nicaragua.

He was a member of the International Conference on American Republics in 1889-90, and he represented the United States on the banking committee and formulated the recommendation for an international American bank. He also reported on the unification of customs regulations and recommended the establishment of a bureau of American republics.

Among other enterprises, he fitted out war vessels in 1889 for the Brazilians who overthrew the Emperor Dom Pedro II; he consolidated the street railways of Syracuse in

1897; he sold the Czar Nicholas 20 submarine and torpedo boats for $35,000,000 in 1904-05, and he acted as negotiator for the Wright Brothers in offering the first practical airplanes to foreign governments in 1908.

His own account of the way the title "Father of Trusts" was given to him, follows: "I made the first speech in favor of organizing industrial consolidations in the eighties," Mr Flint said. "Later, the Chicago newspapers gave me the title of 'Father of Trusts'. When [William Jennings] Bryan was running for the Presidency, Mark Hanna asked me to speak in Chicago before the Illinois Manufacturers Association. McKinley had 500,000 copies of my speech printed and sent throughout the United States."

As to the effect of his organization activities on economic history, Mr Flint said: "I am proud of the act that the combinations that I organized have made money for the subscribers and for the widows and orphans."

Asked if the combination had not also made much for him, Mr Flint said: "No, not so much, because I have always been more interested in the success of the combinations that I organized than in making any large profit. Beyond a certain point, you can't turn cash into comfort or happiness or diversion.

"I did own the fastest sailing yacht in the United States in its time, The Gracie, and later built the fastest steam yacht, The Arrow."

His rule of health was: "Mix sunshine with your blood instead of moonshine. I never took a drink of liquor in my life, because as a member of the Union Club, where drinking was heavy when I was a young man, I saw its effect. I do believe in stimulants when you need them; but by that I mean tea or coffee. I do not drink them regularly, so I have them in reserve."

After his second retirement, he said he proposed to spend the rest of his life driving about and fishing and hunting.

Among the other organizations in which Mr Flint had a hand in putting together were the American-Hawaiian Steamship Company, Autosales Gum and Chocolate Company, the Clarksburg Coal Company, the Computing Scale Company of America, Fairmont Coal Company, International Time Recording Company of New York, National Starch Company, Rubber Goods Manufacturing Company, Sen-Sen Chiclet Company, Sloss-Sheffield Steel and Iron Company, Somerset Coal Company, United States Bobbin and Shuttle Company, and the United States Rubber Company.

Mr Flint was an intimate personal friend of James G. Blaine, and was said to have inspired the reciprocity treaties which Blaine introduced. Mr Blaine often called him to Washington to consult with him on matters affecting the tariff.

40

SAMUEL SACHS (JULY 28, 1851 – MARCH 2, 1935)

THE NEW YORK TIMES, MARCH 3, 1935

*S*amuel Sachs, philanthropist and for many years senior partner in the international banking firm of Goldman, Sachs & Co, died of heart disease early yesterday morning at his residence in the Hotel Pierre, Fifth Avenue and Sixty-first Street. He had been ill only a short time. His age was 83 years.

Mr Sachs's whole life was wrapped up in three major interests - his family, his business and his philanthropies. Among the institutions and organizations of which he was a benefactor were the Montefiore Hospital, Bellevue and Allied Hospitals, the Federation for the Support of Jewish Philanthropic Societies, the Harvard Business School, the Harvard Fine Arts Department and Fisk University at Nashville, Tennessee.

He was born in Baltimore on July 28, 1851, the son of Joseph Sachs and the former Sophia Baer. Before the outbreak of the Civil War, his family moved to this city, where as a young man he entered the mercantile business. He engaged in it for some years before turning to banking.

In 1882, he became associated with his father-in-law,

BLUE MAGPIE BOOKS

Marcus Goldman, in the banking firm which Mr Goldman had founded in 1869. The present name of the firm was adopted not long thereafter. Mr Sachs had been senior partner for many years before his retirement from active participation about seven years ago. Since then, he had been a special partner in the firm.

For a long period of years, Mr Sachs was a director of the Montefiore Hospital. He served as chairman of its finance committee while funds were being raised for the erection of its present building. Mayor William Strong appointed him a trustee of Bellevue and Allied Hospitals, where his work won him wide recognition and reappointment.

Mr Sachs sought to further education in many fields. One of his principal concerns was the education of the Negro, and for years he was a trustee of Fisk University, an institution for members of that race.

On June 17, 1924, the observance of Class Day at Harvard University, it was announced that members of the Sachs family had given $100,000 to the university's Fine Arts Department. Mr Sachs gave $50,000 of this sum, according to the announcement made by Bishop William Lawrence.

At the same time, Bishop Lawrence announced that the firm of Goldman, Sachs & Co was contributing $100,000 to the Harvard Business School. In a letter accompanying this contribution, Mr Sachs said: "Goldman, Sachs & Co are doing this because of their great interest in the development of good management in industrial and commercial companies. It is of primary importance to investors in preferred and common stocks that there be successful management.

"We have realized for years the need of having young men educated for business, not so much in the technical details of business as in the habit of analysis and the reaching of decisions after careful examinations of all available facts.

"We have been in contact with the Harvard Business School for the last three or four years, and have also had the benefit of employing several of the graduates of the school. From our contact and experience with the school, we are confident that the Harvard Business School has already made such progress that it should receive the support of businessmen."

The two contributions made by Mr Sachs and his family at that time were devoted to the $10,000,000 fund which Harvard University was then raising, of which $3,000,000 was to be for chemistry, $2,000,000 for the fine arts and $5,000,000 for the business school.

Mr Sachs served as the chairman of the bankers' and brokers' division of the Business Men's Council in the annual drive of the Federation for the Support of Jewish Philanthropic Societies in 1926-27. In the latter year, that group led all other trade and professional groups, raising pledges totaling $882,787.

In the Fall of 1927, Mr Sachs was appointed a member of the advisory committee to the School of Business of Columbia University. His nomination was made by William L. De Bost, president of the New York State Chamber of Commerce.

Mr Sachs is survived by a widow, Louisa, and by three sons, Paul J. Sachs, Professor of Fine Arts at Harvard University, and Arthur Sachs and Walter E. Sachs, partners of Goldman, Sachs & Co.

The funeral will be private, with only members of the family and a few close friends present. Burial will take place in Salem Fields Cemetery, Brooklyn.

41

EDWARD DOHENY (AUGUST 10, 1856 – SEPTEMBER 8, 1935)

THE NEW YORK TIMES, SEPTEMBER 9, 1935

*L*os Angeles, September 8. Edward Laurence Doheny, who wrested one of the world's largest fortunes from the oil fields of California and Mexico, died at 8 o'clock tonight at his home here. He was 79 years old.

Mr Doheny's death was caused by age and complications after an illness that kept him bedridden for almost three years. At his bedside were his widow, Estelle, and five grandchildren.

Discoverer with the late Charles A. Canfield of one of the first oil fields of California, Mr Doheny had a career that was one of the most picturesque in the history of American industry. In Tampico, Mexico, he reared a vast industrial empire that came to be known as one of the greatest concentrated oil holdings of private capital in the world

Tragedy and sorrow stalked him at the very zenith of his career, however, because of his operations in Elk Hills, California. He was indicted in 1924 in connection with naval reserve leases. Albert B. Fall, former Secretary of the Inte-

rior, also indicted in this case, was convicted, but Mr
Doheny was acquitted.

Only recently, a Doheny-controlled corporation here
foreclosed on the New Mexico ranch of Mr Fall, who
disclosed that he had received orders to vacate. Mr Doheny
and Mr Fall were reported to have remained close friends
through the years, but Doheny made no comment on the
foreclosure.

Edward Laurence Doheny left home when 16 years old
to be a muleteer. He spent the next 20 years tramping plains,
deserts and mountains as a prospector, with the "big strike'*
always just around the corner. In 1892, while walking the
streets of Los Angeles, a mere chance caused him to shift his
quest from gold to petroleum, and a few years later he was
one of the greatest oil operators in the world. He spent his
youth in hardship, his middle age in a phenomenal rise to
wealth, power and fame, and much of his old age in grief
and humiliation through the notorious oil scandals of the
Warren G. Harding administration.

Mr Doheny came of Irish pioneers. He was born on
August 10, 1856, to Patrick and Eleanor Elizabeth (Quigley)
Doheny at Fond du Lac, Wisconsin, which was then in frontier territory. His boyhood surroundings were similar to
those described in the old dime novels. He knew plainsmen
and Indians, and at the early age when he left home to take
charge of the mules in a government surveying expedition
in Indian territory he already knew how to fend for himself.

He saw no future in caring for mules but his trip to the
South-West gave him a taste for the sort of work to which he
was to devote his youth. He had no technical training, but
he observed the government surveyors, picked up the
elements of their trade, and practiced for a while, but soon
decided that it offered little better chances for wealth than

did mule-driving, and it was wealth that Doheny wanted. He talked to prospectors and decided that prospecting was the life for him.

He spent 20 years looking for gold. Sometimes he found it. Repeatedly he built up mines, knew temporary affluence, "went broke" and started out again. The Black Hills of North Dakota lured him. He managed to accumulate a considerable sum of money, organized an expedition, found none of the riches he had dreamed of, and again was poor, with nothing to show for the years of arduous prospecting but a smattering of mining, metallurgy and engineering.

He was in Los Angeles in 1892, nearly penniless, when a Negro unwittingly started him on the road to wealth. The Negro was driving a wagon loaded with a black tarry substance. Doheny asked what was in the wagon. "That's just brear, boss," he was told. Brear is the Mexican word for pitch. "What do you do with it?" the prospector asked. "Oh, they burn it instead of coal," the Negro told him. "Who does?" The Negro told him that it was used in factories and that it came from "a hole out near Westlake Park". Doheny took the first car for Westlake Park and found the hole. He had heard enough about petroleum to be aware that this "brear" was oil-soaked earth. He reasoned that if the earth at the surface was oily, there must be an oil deposit close below. But he had no money.

He encountered an old friend, a fellow prospector named Charles Canfield, who also lacked funds. Despite their financial handicap, the two men managed to lease a vacant lot near Westlake Park. Neither had had any experience in oil, so they set about "mining" it as they had mined gold. They sank a shaft 150 feet and struck a little oil. From this they got money enough to go down further. One day, when their shaft had sunk 225 feet, something happened, and wealth spouted out of the ground in a high gusher. The great Los Angeles oil boom was on.

Hundreds of competitors poured in and there followed a furious scramble for land on which to drill. Moreover, Doheny and Canfield had no place to store their petroleum. As fast as they could, they constructed crude wooden tanks, each holding about 100 barrels. Their competitors brought in skilled oil men and Doheny and Canfield found themselves under a severe handicap. Within two years, more than 200 companies had drilled 2,300 wells in Los Angeles and the city had made rapid strides toward its present eminence. Doheny had not yet achieved wealth on the scale of which he dreamed, but at least he had acquired capital.

He decided that the way to put it to its best use was to find and develop a new oil field. Old records indicate that the early Spaniards and the Indians before them were aware of the existence of oil in the Tampico section of Mexico. At the beginning of the 20th century, oil had not become the liquid gold of its later history, and although it was even then a potential source of wealth, nobody had done anything about the deposits around Tampico. In his early prospecting days, Doheny had visited Mexico. He liked the Mexicans and he knew how to get along with them. Accordingly, he arranged his affairs in Los Angeles and set forth to find a world to conquer.

He landed in Tampico in 1900. It was a village at the mouth of the narrow Pánuco River, which wound into the Gulf of Mexico out of the hot, tangled green of the jungle. The oil operator, a prospector once more, outfitted a little expedition, hired an Indian to guide him and headed into the jungle. There was a place where a black fluid that would burn flowed out of the earth, the Indian told him; and 10 miles further on was a lake of the same fluid. The Indian promised to lead him to it and made good the promise.

Doheny returned to the United States with leases on 1,000,000 acres of Mexican land and a dream of a great corporation. Home again, he organized the Mexican Petroleum Company with a capitalization of $10,000,000. Ships began to arrive in Tampico with men, equipment and supplies. Warehouses were erected, roads were constructed, railroads were laid down, and the jungle gave way before man's search for one of the great oil centres of the world.

Doheny dominated the Tampico field and later the Tuxpan field, the first a great producer of heavy oil, the second turning out huge quantities of a lighter oil with high gasoline content. The total production ran to millions of barrels a month. Doheny had built an oil empire.

Controversies have raged about the part he played in Mexican politics. Many Mexicans held that he was taking what rightfully belonged to the Mexican Government and people. His name was linked with revolutionary movements, and in 1921 he was accused by General Manuel Peláez of fomenting a revolt at Tampico. That his large holdings should make him a storm centre in a troubled country was inevitable, but just what part he played in the various disturbances has not been established.

His difficulties were not confined to Mexico. His stock was a centre of interest on the New York Stock Exchange. He was at one time called before the governors and asked to explain the unusual fluctuations in its market price. He convinced them that he had made no "corner", as contended by some.

It was in his old age that Doheny had to withstand some of the hardest blows of his career. When the oil scandals of the Harding Administration became known in 1924, he was accused of having given $100,000 to Albert B. Fall, Harding's Secretary of the Interior, as a bribe in connection with the lease of the Elk Hills naval oil reserves. During the seemingly endless litigation, civil and criminal, Doheny consistently maintained that he had given the money as a loan in consideration of his friendship of long standing with Fall. He saw Fall, with whom he had prospected in his earlier days, sentenced to prison for accepting the bribe. He stood in the courtroom at the time and tried to comfort his old friend.

Despite this conviction and the finding by the United States Supreme Court in a unanimous decision that the Elk Hills lease as well as other transactions in which Doheny, Fall, Harry F. Sinclair and others were concerned was full of fraud and corruption, in March 1930, a jury found Doheny not guilty of bribing Fall. He had been indicted six years earlier.

During the years of public attack, he maintained that he had not tried to swindle his country but had acted on motives of patriotism. At the height of the scandals in which his name figured so prominently, his only son, Edward L. Doheny Jr, was murdered by a servant. His son had brought the $100,000 to Fall in "a little black satchel", and during one of the many proceedings the mention of his son's name caused him to weep on the witness stand.

In February 1932, the United States Circuit Court in San Francisco canceled the $12,000,000 Kern County naval oil reserve leases to the Pan-American Petroleum Company, a Doheny concern, in a decision imputing the leases to the Fall "bribe". Later in the same year, conspiracy indictments naming Mr Doheny and others were dropped and the criminal cases resulting from the oil scandals of the Harding administration were ended.

In recent years, Mr Doheny had lived in virtual retirement, so far as the public was concerned. In 1933 and again in 1934, there were reports from Los Angeles that Mr Doheny had received extortion demands on pain of "grave danger".

Doheny's life was one of ups and downs, successes and failures, poverty and enormous wealth, great success and great tragedy. He was, in a sense, one of America's "empire-builders". He made cities out of towns, and made towns where before there had been wilderness. He built railroads and tanker lines and extended the frontiers of civilization. His motto was "Never look back".

Outside of matters linked directly with his business, he had a major interest in the establishment of an Irish republic. In April 1921, at Chicago, he was elected president of the American Association for the Recognition of the Irish Republic. He was reported to have underwritten a $4,000,000 fund for the relief of the Irish and was said to have been America's largest contributor of money to the cause of a free Ireland.

In appearance he was slight, with a suggestion of a stoop in his shoulders. His eyes were blue-gray and he had a gray mustache. His mannerisms as well as his way of speaking suggested the quick and impulsive. He dressed modestly and always avoided long-tail coats and top hats. His wife was Carrie Estelle Betzold, of Marshalltown, Iowa.

He was president of the Pan-American Western Petroleum Company, the Petroleum Securities Company, the Mexican Petroleum Company of California, and the Doheny-Stone Drill Company, and chairman of the Pan-American Petroleum Company of California. During the war, he was a member of the subcommittee on oil of the Council of National Defense. Mr Doheny sold the Pan-

American Western to the Richfield Oil Company of California in 1928. This deal was followed by considerable litigation. He was a member of the California and the Jonathan Club of Los Angeles, the Bohemian Club of San Francisco and the Union League Club of Chicago. A keen yachtsman, he belonged to the Atlantic Yacht Club of Brooklyn, of which he was the commodore; the Columbia Yacht Club here and the California Yacht Club of Los Angeles.

42

JOHN HAYS HAMMOND (MARCH 31, 1855 – JUNE 8, 1936)

THE CHARLESTON DAILY MAIL, WEST VIRGINIA, JUNE 9, 1936

*J*ohn Hays Hammond Sr, a Californian who started on a shoestring and became a multi-millionaire mining expert, died suddenly of heart disease at his palatial estate, Lookout Hill, late yesterday. He was 81. The man who had been the friend and confidant of presidents, empire builders and just plain miners died in his study while reading.

Hammond had been in ill health for a year, but he arrived at Lookout Hill Saturday from Washington apparently in much better health. He took an active part in superintending the opening of his estate for the summer season. Death came to Hammond just as an old friend, Mrs Edward M. House, wife of Colonel House, one-time advisor to Former President Woodrow Wilson, called to visit him.

If the life story of Mr Hammond, gold prospector, mining expert, multi-millionaire and adventurer, could be written into a motion picture or a popular novel, it probably would make a place well up in the ranks of thrillers.

Attacked by Mexican bandits; saved from an ignoble death at the end of a Boer rope in the Transvaal; jumping from poverty to wealth; seeking adventure from one side of the globe to the other - these were only a few of the instances in the active life of one of the world's best known and most able engineers.

Occupant of vermin-ridden shacks on the frontiers of the earth, he was also the silk-hatted special ambassador of the president of the United States to the Court of St James. At one time too poor to hire an office boy, he later named his own fees for his services. His friends ranged from the wooly gold miners and plainsmen of the Far West to kings, princes and emperors. He was a close personal friend of Theodore Roosevelt; knew Mark Twain, Rudyard Kipling and Rider Haggard; was the confident of Cecil Rhodes and "Barney" Barnato; and was received bv the last Czar of Russia. Yet through all his varied career, Mr Hammond remained a quiet, unassuming American citizen.

His ancestry and the surroundings in which Mr Hammond spent his youth, were such as to stir the spirit of adventure in any boy. His forebears were among the early and notable settlers of this country. His father, a native of Maryland and a graduate of West Point, served as a major in the war with Mexico. His mother, a Tennessean, was the sister of Colonel John Hay, famous in the early history of Texas.

As a boy, he rubbed shoulders with the sturdy gold miners of his home state, and used to spend his vacations with them, watching them pan gravel and dirt. At 10, he was a practiced hunter and sure shot.

He early showed an aptitude for mineralogy, and, after public and private schooling, his father sent him to Yale, where he was graduated in 1876 with the degree of Bachelor of Philosophy. from the Sheffield Scientific School. Yale later conferred upon him the degree of Master of Arts.

In 1911, President William Howard Taft appointed Mr Hammond special ambassador and personal representative at the coronation of King George V. His name was offered as nominee for vice-president with Taft but was rejected. He was high in Republican party circles and served a term as president of the National League of Republican Clubs.

In 1912, he was president of the Panama-Pacific Exposition commission that visited Europe in the interests of the great organization. In 1915 and 1916, he was chairman of the World Court Congress, and in 1922 President Warren G. Harding appointed him to the United States Coal Commission erected to investigate the coal industry after the mine strike of that year. His associates elected him chairman of the body.

In 1880, Mr Hammond married Miss Natalie Harris, of Mississippi. Three children were born to them, and John Hays Hammond Jr, who inherited much of his father's scientific genius, became a brilliant inventor before reaching his 30th year.

43

HENRY WELLCOME (AUGUST 21, 1853 – JULY 25, 1936)

THE NEW YORK TIMES, JULY 26, 1936

*L*ondon, July 25. - Sir Henry Solomon Wellcome, the scientist who was born near Milwaukee and became a princely benefactor of British medical research, died here today, after an operation, at the age of 82.

Born in a log cabin in a frontier settlement in Wisconsin, Henry S. Wellcome, in his long career, came to be one of the world's noted scientists and explorers. As a boy of six, he held a basin while his uncle, Dr J.W.B. Wellcome, dressed the wounds of Minnesota pioneers who had been in battle with the Indians.

After the World War, during the course of which he became a British subject by naturalization, he himself pioneered in another field, that of archaeological exploration by airplane.

Knighted in 1932 by King George for his services to medicine and pharmaceutical development, Sir Henry was the founder of the Wellcome Research Institution in London, the Wellcome Historical Medical Museum and the Wellcome Bureau of Scientific Research. He also founded, in 1927, the Lady Stanley Maternity Hospital and, earlier, the

Wellcome Medical Hospital Dispensary in Uganda, Central Africa, both being under the control of the Medical Mission of the Church Missionary Society.

He was himself the son of an itinerant missionary, the Rev S.C. Wellcome, who with Sir Henry's mother, Mary Curtis Wellcome, traveled and preached in a covered wagon in Wisconsin and Minnesota. Sir Henry served as a drug clerk in Rochester, Minnesota, from 1868 to 1871 and always attributed his success in after life to the interest of Dr William W. Mayo, father of the Mayo brothers of Rochester. The elder Dr Mayo arranged for the matriculation of young Wellcome at the Philadelphia School of Pharmacy and Chemistry.

Sir Henry became the head of Burroughs, Wellcome and Company of London, manufacturers of chemicals, with establishments in the United States, Italy, Canada, Australia, India, China and other countries. His American interests were wide and varied. He was a director of the Gorgas Memorial Institute of Tropical and Preventive Medicine at Washington, which operates research laboratories at Panama. In 1910, at the instance of the Secretary of War, Jacob M. Dickinson, he made a detailed inspection of the operations in the Canal Zone and heartily endorsed the work done there by General William C. Gorgas.

Knowing the American Indian from first-hand contact as a boy, Sir Henry maintained his interest in the Red Man. For many years, he took a close interest in the welfare of a tribe of Indians in Alaska and in 1887 published a book of 500 pages on this tribe under the title *The Story of Metlakahtla*. Archaeological interests, which were later to receive world-wide recognition, were also aroused in Sir Henry by his early experiences.

In one of the expeditions which he led in 1901 in the

Upper Nile regions of the Anglo-Egyptian Sudan, he discovered several prehistoric Ethiopian sites. Excavations were carried out under his personal direction and the results were fruitful. The extent of the work may be realized from the fact that he employed a staff of 25 Europeans and more than 3,000 native workmen.

These archaeological undertakings were resumed in 1910 and extensive work was done, but the operations were temporarily interrupted by the outbreak of the war. Sir Henry placed the services of his Bureau of Scientific Research in London and its staff at the disposal of the British Government and they were used by the War Office. He also instituted a special commission to secure improvements in the design and construction of field ambulances. He constructed and supplied to the British Army Medical Service a chemical and bacteriological motor field research laboratory used in Palestine and Egypt during the war

Sir Henry's interest in preventative medicine reached to all corners of the world. He was the founder of a Publication Trust Fund under the control and direction of the Chinese Medical Association to provide standard medical, surgical and chemical textbooks translated into Chinese at prices within reach of native students. He was a member of the Central Asian Society and of the Council of the African Society, an Officer of the Order of St John of Jerusalem, life member of the National Geographic Society, Washington, and the Minnesota Historical Society, and past honorary president of the American Pharmaceutical Association, to which he had belonged since 1875.

He was also a member of the American Oriental Society and an honorary member of the American Society for Tropical Medicine and of the Association of Military Surgeons of the United States. He was vice-president of the Royal

Anthropological Institute; vice-president and member of council, Royal Society of Arts; fellow of the Royal Society of Medicine and Royal Society of Tropical Medicine and Hygiene, London; corresponding member of the Ancient College of Doctors of Medicine of Madrid.

Sir Henry was fellow of the Society of Antiquaries, Royal Geographical Society, Zoological Society, a member of the Royal Institution, the executive committee of the governing board, Gordon Memorial College, Khartoum, and honorary vice-president of the Society for Nautical Research, London.

He held the Cross of Chevalier of the Legion of Honor and was a Freeman of the Ancient Worshipful Society of Apothecaries of the City of London. In 1928, he received the honorary degree of Doctor of Laws from Edinburgh University.

44

JOHN D. ROCKEFELLER SR (JULY 8, 1839 – MAY 23, 1937)

THE TIMES OF INDIA, MAY 24, 1937

*T*o Scottish blood belongs the distinction of having produced the wealthiest two men of the United States, Mr John D. Rockefeller and Mr Andrew Carnegie. By repute, Mr Rockefeller was also the richest man of the world. He never claimed that exalted place in plutocracy and discouraged references to it, which made the general public, especially the American, all the more persistent in spreading the reputation.

It was Mr Rockefeller's great ambition to live to be 100. For that purpose, he began to lead for the last few years a quiet and sequestered life. His physicians made him give up all physical exertion. Golf, for long a favourable pastime, was foregone. Christmas parties and other entertainments which taxed him were stopped, and the sight of Mr Rockefeller, seated in one of his motor cars and warmly wrapped up in rugs, was a rare one. Complete relaxation, mental and physical, it was hoped would bring him to his greatest ambition, according to the doctors, but all the resources of science failed to do so. He would have completed 99 years on July 8 next.

He never took the public into his confidence as to the approximate value of his riches, but he occasionally hinted that he was not as wealthy as most persons thought. The American public accepted that as another instance of Mr Rockefeller's "shyness" or "modesty", which for many years had made the Oil King a shining example among the silent capitalists of America. But as Mr Rockefeller advanced in age and the American people began to grow more demonstrative in their efforts to ascertain how certain mammoth fortunes were obtained, he became quite loquacious, said he wished to be better understood and talked of almost everything except his own wealth and the exact methods by which he acquired it.

Aside from the marvellous power of money-making, no phases of Mr Rockefeller's career were more interesting than his exhibitions of moral courage and self-control under an avalanche of vituperation that descended upon him for many years. He apparently never flinched under the weight of popular odium, even when his physical condition was at a very low ebb, and harsh words from his lips, if ever spoken, never reached the public.

Granted that the founder of the greatest commercial Trust the world had ever seen crushed competition by unfair means, there was much in his personal attitude toward the public that commanded a peculiar sympathy on the part of many persons who came into contact with Mr Rockefeller in religious, charitable and educational circles.

In spite of the widespread movement against the acceptance of "tainted money" by religious, charitable, and educational institutions, there were comparatively few which declined to receive the Oil King's aid. The demands upon his charity became so great that he was forced to organise a corps of investigators and consultants for the distribution of his money gifts. These were generally of a conditional character, that is, the institutions were to raise certain sums before they could get what Mr Rockefeller offered. In all of his charities, he displayed remarkable business acumen. Mr Rockefeller did not divulge the full extent of his charities. His largest gifts, of course, became known, but he dispensed many millions which did not.

Mr Rockefeller gave a fairly complete description of his early life in informal talks to young men's Bible classes in Baptist Churches of New York City and Cleveland, Ohio. He dwelt less on his parentage than he did on his own early training. His parents settled on a small farm, at Richford, New York State, several years before he was born on July 8, 1839. His father, William Avery Rockefeller, was a genial, but somewhat mysterious character, fond of hunting, a horse-trader, nomadic and somewhat irreligious. It is also stated that he was a "quack doctor". His mother was a strict disciplinarian, very religious and far-seeing.

In talking of his boyhood, John D. Rockefeller said to a Bible class in New York: "It seemed to be a business training from the very beginning. I was taught to do things - simple things such as a boy could do. I was taught to be self-reliant, at the age of seven or eight I was taught to milk a cow. I could milk a cow as well as a man could. It was simple but important. I was taught at the age of eight to drive a horse, and drive him just as carefully as a man could drive him - I shall never forget that I was taught to do as much business at the age of 10 and 11 as it was possible for me to do. Among other things, I was sent over the hills to buy cord wood for the use of the family."

After relating how he earned money in digging potatoes for a neighbour, Mr Rockefeller continued: "As I was saving these little sums, I soon learned that I could get as much interest for $50 loaned at seven per cent - the legal rate in the State of New York at that time - as I could earn by digging potatoes for 10 days. The impression was gaining ground with me that it was a good thing to let the money be my slave and not make myself a slave to money. I've tried to remember that in every sense. I think money is a good thing to have if we know how to use it properly. My parents kept me at school until I was 16 years old. I had expected to go through college and enjoy the advantage that many of you gentlemen have enjoyed, but I cannot say that I regret that circumstance seemed to require me to begin to take care of myself."

Mr Rockefeller described how at the outset of his career he obtained employment in a general commission house through the aid of an acquaintance. Just before he became 19, he decided to engage in the produce business in partnership with a young man. He had saved a large part of his wages - several thousand dollars - and his father, whose financial means had improved, lent him a small sum at 10 per cent interest until he should become of age. The conditions of the loan made Mr Rockefeller's auditors laugh.

After several years' experience of conducting a commission business, Mr Rockefeller became restless. He was not making money fast enough, A friend told him that there was a splendid financial future in the petroleum trade. Mr Rockefeller, with two partners, one of whom soon withdrew, built a small oil refinery from which the great Standard Oil Company developed. A few years after entering the petroleum business, Mr Rockefeller's brother, William, joined him.

The firm lacked sufficient capital and creditors began to harass them. William Rockefeller became despondent. John D. appeared at the refinery one morning carrying a valise.

"Where are you going?" inquired Mr Andrews, a member of the firm. "I am going to get help" was the reply.

John D. Rockefeller searched for a couple of weeks for aid and finally met a wealthy citizen of Michigan, S.V. Harkness, whose son-in-law, Henry M. Flagler, was not doing very well in the salt and lumber business. Mr Rockefeller pointed out the advantages of the petroleum trade. Mr Harkness decided to invest £12,000 in the Rockefeller firm and place his son-in-law in control of the interest.

This was the pivotal point in the fortunes of the Rockefellers and also of Mr Flagler, who developed remarkable talents in the petroleum trade. In 1870, the firm had become so prosperous that it was deemed best to incorporate the business as the Standard Oil Company. In the meantime, Mr Andrews had withdrawn from the firm and had received £200,000 for his interest. The launching of the Oil Corporation was followed by consolidations. Small oil refiners either voluntarily or involuntarily sold out to the great business machine, which the Rockefellers and Mr Flagler developed.

In 1882, an Oil Trust was formed and 10 years later after it had gained a monopoly of the trade, it was "dissolved" following the decision of the Supreme Court of Ohio that it was illegal.

Mr Rockefeller practically retired from business in 1898. He rarely visited the Standard Oil Offices in New York City after that date. While he remained the nominal head of the great business, he gave very little attention to it, but devoted his time to the building of his health, which had been nearly shattered through his severe application to work, and to charitable and church work. Dyspepsia had seized him in its most violent form. All the hairs of his head dropped out and in his last years he wore a wig. To bicycling and golf he owed his recovery in health, after eight years of endeavour. It was the greatest struggle of his life.

As long as he was actively engaged in business, Mr Rockefeller was the presiding genius of the Standard Oil Company. He had a remarkable grasp of details and what may be termed a mania for effecting economies. The various methods by which waste was prevented in the conduct of the great business enterprise under the leadership of Mr Rockefeller stamped him as a man of extraordinary ingenuity. He also had the valuable faculty of being able to select able lieutenants. The Standard Oil "crowd", as it was termed, was considered the shrewdest body of men ever engaged in any one business in America.

Mr Rockefeller never claimed the larger share of credit for the upbuilding of the Standard Oil Company. He invariably distributed the credit with lavishness upon his associates. He exercised no imperial sway, but ruled in a quiet and persuasive manner. Among the great army of Standard Oil employees, his face was not familiar, except through the pictures published in newspapers. The organisation under his direction was almost as impersonal as that of machinery.

In private life, Mr Rockefeller was affable and courteous. There was nothing either in his dress or demeanour suggestive of the "new rich". He dressed plainly, rarely referred to his wealth - in such cases, the references were usually induced by questions - and associated with those identified with the religious and educational worlds.

His most conspicuous activity, outside of business, was in Church work and was devoted to the Baptist denomination. Mr Rockefeller was always held in the highest esteem in Baptist circles.

Mr Rockefeller neither drank liquor nor used tobacco.

He cared nothing for "fashionable" society. He did not attend the theatre or the opera. He did not fill his residences with "costly" paintings - a form of expenditure which so many wealthy Americans have adopted for the disposal of part of their surplus riches.

The dominant note of Mr Rockefeller's life was that of a hard-headed, shrewd and calculating business man without love of art or, apparently, of beauty in many of its forms.

When he was in his early twenties, Mr Rockefeller married Miss Lucy Spelman, a school teacher of Cleveland, Ohio. They had five children, a son, John D. Jr, and four daughters. The bulk of Mr Rockefeller's fortune will undoubtedly go to his son, who has undergone a long training to assume the burden of the vast wealth.

45

ANDREW MELLON (MARCH 24, 1855 – AUGUST 26, 1937)

MIAMI DAILY NEWS RECORD, OKLAHOMA, AUGUST 27, 1937

*A*ndrew W. Mellon, who built one of the world's greatest fortunes out of banking, oil and aluminum, and who spent his late years in the nation's service as secretary of the Treasury and as ambassador to Great Britain, has passed from the American scene. The shy, diffident, white-haired financier, whose 11 years of service under three Presidents was surpassed only by one of his predecessors as head of the Treasury department, died peacefully last night in his eighty-third year.

Mellon was fabulously wealthy, but the extent of his personal fortune was in the realm of speculation when he died. The only official estimate made public was $205,000,000, given by Mellon's secretary during hearing of the banker's income tax appeal in 1931. Friends said, however, they believed the combined fortune of the financier and his two children would amount to approximately $500,000,000.

Like John D. Rockefeller Sr, and other contemporaries, Mellon's personal fortune had been partly dissipated by the lavishness of his philanthropies. Mellon's vast enterprises reached around the earth and gave employment to thousands. Banking, oil and aluminum were his principal interests and their corporate names were the Mellon National Bank of Pittsburgh, one of the nation's largest, the Gulf Oil company, and the Aluminum Company of America, dominant in its field.

Only a few weeks before his last illness, he visited President Franklin D. Roosevelt and made final arrangements for his last great public benefaction - establishment of a national gallery of art in the national capital with his $50,000,000 art collection, one of the finest extant, as the nucleus.

One of the last great statesmen-financiers of the nation, Andrew William Mellon successfully shunned the limelight and was little known to his countrymen until he became secretary of the Treasury under President Warren G. Harding in 1921. He remained on the job until 1932, when he retired to become ambassador to Great Britain.

Fellow Republicans hailed him as "the greatest secretary of the Treasury since Alexander Hamilton", but he was the target of sharp attack by the Democrats, who unsuccessfully attempted to drive him from office in 1924. He was proud of his record as a cabinet officer and his party cited the reduction in the public debt from $23,737,000,000 in 1921 to $17,820,000,000 during his service. He met the criticism that the public debt had been reduced too rapidly with the statement that "far from hurting the country, it has been a great benefit to all those who needed capital".

Mellon retired to private life in 1933 when he resigned as ambassador to Great Britain, and afterwards seldom appeared in public. A man of few words who left speech-making to others, his last public speech was at the dedication of the new home of the Mellon Institute of Industrial

Research in Pittsburgh on May 6. Mellon, who with his brother, Richard, established the institute in 1913 to conduct scientific research in industry, said on this occasion that "new discoveries and inventions" - not governmental or political action - have been responsible for "increased production, lowered costs, raised wages and a higher standard of living".

Born to wealth, Andrew Mellon was a man of simple tastes, a multi-millionaire who never owned a yacht, a private Pullman car, or a country estate.

Mellon's public record crowned a lengthy career as a banker in which he built up one of the great fortunes of this world. But it brought him also into a whirl of politics, making him a shining mark for opposition critics. There was an abortive attempt to indict him in 1934 on charges of evading income tax, and when this failed he had to answer before the board of tax appeals in Washington a claim by the government for alleged shortages in his 1931 return, the claim including allegations of fraud and evasion. But Mellon, a shy, imperturbable little man, given to slow speech, was a fighter, and he hit back lustily.

Mellon's Treasury career was notable for its handling of difficult post-war financial problems, including refunding agreements with 13 debtor European nations; tax reductions; a cut of 20 per cent in America's national debt, and the fact that under his guidance the United States, of all the nations engaged in the World War, was the first to attain a balanced budget after that conflict. He assumed the secretaryship when President Harding took office on March 4, 1921, and held it under Presidents Calvin Coolidge and Herbert Hoover until February 5, 1932, when the Senate confirmed his nomination as ambassador to Great Britain.

Only one other head of department exceeded the length

of this service, Albert Gallatin holding this post under Presidents Thomas Jefferson and James Madison, from 1801 to the spring of 1813. Another secretary, William Windom, held office under three Presidents, but there was a lapse between his brief service under Presidents James Garfield and Chester A. Arthur and his two years under President Benjamin Harrison in 1889.

Mellon stepped into the Treasury when the government's financial affairs were in a gloomy state, resulting largely from a depression which followed the inflationary boom during and immediately after the war. Tax rates were the highest in history and the internal revenue laws, hurriedly drawn to bring in war funds, constantly were objects of litigation. The way he handled the task of financial reconstruction has been compared by numerous admirers to the administration of Alexander Hamilton, first secretary of the Treasury, who faced similar grave problems.

His tax reduction program, involving a decrease of about 30 per cent in the maximum surtaxes on incomes, was assailed as favouring the rich, and his insistence on the settlement of war debts by foreign nations was criticized at home and abroad, but he saw most of his plans adopted. By 1926, he had cut the public debt by around $6,000,000,000 from about $26,000,000,000.

Unschooled in practical politics, Mellon was the target for repeated attacks in Congress, but he went about his work generally heedless of detractors and seldom took public notice of their charges. The differences arose on subjects ranging from taxation, prohibition enforcement, the soldiers' bonus, war debt settlements and farm relief, to charges that he was a representative of big business and was holding office in violation of a law prohibiting the secretary of the Treasury from engaging in trade. Twice efforts were made to remove him, but his position proved unassailable.

His attitude on prohibition was, including refunding agreements, a realistic one. Although devoting much thought to a reorganization of prohibition enforcement on a more efficient basis, he pointed out in his annual reports the great difficulties of attempting to make the "wet" states "dry" against their wishes

Mellon's first demand for reduction of heavy surtaxes failed to obtain congressional support, being opposed even by some of the administration leaders. Turning to the people, however, he won approval that meant passage of his revenue bill in 1926.

A mere tyro in political maneuvering when he entered the cabinet, his years of service as head of the government finances made him astute in that phase of American life. At the 1928 Republican national convention, when the "stop-Hoover" movement was at its height, he was instrumental in swinging the Pennsylvania delegation to the Hoover column at a strategic moment, thus assuring the Californian's nomination.

Of Irish Protestant stock, he was born on March 24, 1854, at Pittsburgh, the fourth of six sons of Judge Thomas and Sarah Jane Negley Mellon. His father was judge in the Allegheny county court, and retired from the bench in 1869 to establish the banking house of T. Mellon & Sons.

Andrew Mellon was educated in a private school and in the University of Pittsburgh, class of 1873, leaving college shortly before commencement. The next year, he entered his father's banking house and was made a partner a year later. When his father retired from business in 1887, Andrew became the senior of the firm.

The partnership, including his brother, Richard B.

Mellon, entered the national banking system in July 1902 as the Mellon National bank. With Andrew Mellon as president, it grew into one of the most important banks in the country. He resigned the presidency of the institution three days before he entered the cabinet, and also gave up all his other business connections.

In 1889, the brothers and associates organised the Union Trust company and the Union Savings Bank of Pittsburgh. Three other banks and a trust company later came under Mellon control, the total resources being in excess of $500,000,000. The industrial interests into many fields, including aluminum, coal, iron, oil and shipping, until some estimators put at nearly $8,000,000,000 the total worth of the enterprises in which Mellon and his brothers had a voice.

How much of that total was the individual property of Andrew Mellon was problematical. One gauge of his personal fortune was furnished by the Democratic administration's attacks on his income tax returns. The tax board case revealed that he had filed a return showing a gross income of $10,890,485 in 1931, but the government claimed this total should have been $13,482,660. He paid a tax of $647,559, the return showing a net income of $1,927,116 with capital losses on stock sales of more than $6,500,000 and gifts and charitable contributions of $3,821,178 as the chief deduction items. The government disputed both of these items and claimed an additional tax of $2,050,068 plus 50 per cent of that amount as penalty.

The task of building up and managing the huge fortune which these figures mirrored gave Mellon little time for interests outside his office. He was 45 years old before he married and he was 67 when he entered the cabinet. He found relaxation in a little golf, an occasional horseback ride and by walking to and from his work. He took annual trips abroad to indulge his hobby for art and his collection of paintings was one of the best in America.

His marriage was contracted to Nora McMullen at Hartford, England, on September 12, 1900. A daughter, Ailsa, who married David K.E. Bruce, and a son, Paul, were born to them. The union ended in divorce in 1910, the children remaining with their father when the Senate confirmed his nomination as ambassador to Great Britain.

46

ABE BAILEY (NOVEMBER 6, 1864 – AUGUST 10, 1940)

THE TIMES OF LONDON, AUGUST 12, 1940

*S*ir Abe Bailey, for upwards of half a century one of the most vigorous personalities in South African public life, died on Saturday at his Muizenberg house, near Cape Town, at the age of 75, telegraphs our Cape Town Correspondent.

Nothing but the most remarkable courage and vitality preserved his life so long, for within the last three years he had suffered the amputation of both his legs, and many men would have surrendered at once to so grievous an ending of an unusually active career. But he never allowed his misfortune to interrupt his many interests or his delight in the society of his friends. Till last autumn he made his customary journeys between England and South Africa, maintained all his associations in both countries, and kept his spirits high.

In his earlier years, he had two reputations. He was a Rand magnate, and there was no more sagacious or daring speculator on the Rand than "Abe". At the same time, he was a sportsman in various fields, and notably on the Turf, who achieved distinction both in this country and in his own. He was himself a good cricketer, a footballer, a keen boxer and shot. In South Africa, he had long been looked up to as the Maecenas of both professional and amateur games-players. He selected cricketers as his private secretaries. He brought out a noted professional to give tone to Johannesburg golf. More than once he had helped a promising young sportsman of scant means to a career at the university or in mining. It was due to Bailey that a team of South African cricketers came to England in 1904, to spring on us the puzzling "googly". From that visit evolved the "triangular" contests between the Old Country, South Africa, and the Australians.

But sport, although a dominant expression of Bailey's restless, robust mind, was only one of his manifold activities. In mining, he had not perhaps the patience by which a good "prospect" is developed, equipped with costly plant, and brought to fruition in actual gold production and profits. Bailey would throw out his engineers far afield, like scouts; on their report, he would take up and test the "good things" which others perhaps had passed by. The share market, always interested in Bailey's movements, would take a hand. A sharp rise in values often enabled Bailey to dispose of his holdings at a spectacular profit and leave to others the work of bringing a brilliant prospect to the producing stage. Actual "Bailey" mines producing gold and paying dividends have therefore been few and far between, and for that reason "Abe", while an undoubted Rand magnate, never achieved or desired the solid dignity of an established "mining house".

Thus it was with unusual freedom from business cares and an exceptionally solid basis of cash that Bailey had the time and the means to become a large landowner, a successful farmer, and a politician who was anything but a meek party man. He was a keen, progressive farmer. He had excellent imported stock from Home on his group of farms in the Colesberg district of Cape Colony. In politics, he modelled himself deliberately on Cecil Rhodes as his ideal of a good South African and a devoted Imperialist.

A "White South Africa", *sans phrase*, was the slogan which he untiringly enunciated, and he meant it. He was therefore a consistent opponent of the Indian propaganda in Natal and the Transvaal and the claims of Indians to equal rights in trading and the ownership of land. Sir Abe exercised considerable influence through his interest in two leading Johannesburg newspapers, the *Rand Daily Mail* and the *Sunday Times*. In British politics, he was a strong supporter of Imperial Preference, and he made liberal donations also in aid of the campaign for Tariff Reform. Without pretensions to oratory, he could make a clear, earnest speech. Although it cannot be said that the mantle of Rhodes fell either on him or indeed on any other South African, Bailey's loyalty to the memory of the Colossus was as a secret monitor to whom he might have recourse for guidance. Hardy materialist as he was in some respects, some fine and little-known actions are known to have had their origin in his self-questioning: "What would Rhodes have done?"

Hence, perhaps the touch of greatness which this forceful personality brought to the handling of life. Hence, too, the munificence of his support for causes which he felt that Rhodes would have approved. He had much the same admiration for Lord Alfred Milner and remained to the end a close friend of "Milner's young men". Among his many benefactions were £100,000 to the Royal Institute of International Affairs, for research; £2,000 for the preservation of Cecil Rhodes's birthplace at Bishop's Stortford; and two gifts totalling £15,000 for the encouragement of civil aviation in South Africa and in Southern and Northern Rhodesia.

Like so many of the outstanding South African English, Bailey was an "Eastern Province" man. He was born on November 6, 1864, at Cradock, a little town in a prosperous sheep-raising district. His father, the Hon Thomas Bailey, a Yorkshireman from the West Riding, was a well-to-do general storekeeper who became member for Queenstown in the Cape Legislative Assembly. After receiving his schooling at Clewer House, Windsor, young Bailey returned to South Africa in 1881 and joined his father in business.

About four years later, tired of the steady-going life of the "Old Colony", he trekked to the faraway new goldfields at Barberton, in the Eastern Transvaal. There, he started in business as a stockbroker, and tasted the first joys of speculation. Three years later, Barberton was emptied of its adventurous spirits by the rush to the Rand, then in the first fever of new discovery and wild gambling in claims and shares. At Johannesburg, Bailey resumed his stockbroking, which in those days meant buying and selling shares, incidentally for any client that presented themselves, but largely for the stockbroker himself. In the great "boom" of 1895, Bailey laid the foundations of his fortune solidly, and acquired the nucleus of that hard cash which he utilized to such effect later on both in his daring speculative deals and in his public work. Success enabled him to leave his various interests in the care of competent managers and to travel and change his residence from South Africa to England and back again at will.

As a member of the Reform Committee which voiced the Uitlander grievances, Bailey was "in" the Raid in 1896, and in the rising at Johannesburg with which the Uitlander population at Johannesburg attempted to aid Dr Jameson's invasion of the Transvaal. After the defeat and capture of Jameson by President Kruger's commandos, Bailey, with the other principal Reformers - save a few who fled the country - was arrested and brought to trial in Pretoria. A sentence of two years' imprisonment was commuted to a fine together with an undertaking to abstain from further political agitation.

When the South African War came, Bailey bestirred himself actively. Attached to Lord Roberts's staff, he saw service in the main advance. He raised Gorringe's Horse, one of the numerous irregular corps mainly manned by the Uitlanders, and, in this country, helped in mounting and equipping the City Imperial Volunteers for service in South Africa.

When peace was signed and the Transvaal safely placed under Crown Colony government, Bailey found an opening for a political debut at the Cape. Under the banner of Dr Jameson, who as Premier united the various Progressive parties, Bailey was returned to the Assembly for Barkly West, Rhodes's old constituency. The organizing ability and aspirations of the recruit from the Rand were recognized by his appointment as Whip to the Progressive Party. He, however, resigned when the Transvaal was granted self-government, and transferred his political ambitions to the more stimulating and familiar atmosphere of the Rand.

Here, he obtained a seat in the Legislative Assembly at Pretoria, and took up his old office as Whip to the Progressive (British) Party. He sat as representative of Krugersdorp, the "capital" of the West Rand, where he had active mining interests.

The inclusion of the Transvaal and Orange Free State among self-governing States within the Empire gave immediate impetus to the ideal of a Union of all the four South African Colonies in a single Dominion. With the financial support of Bailey, *The State*, a review of a type new in South African journalism, popularized the case for closer union with admirable vigour and tenacity. On the consummation of Union, Bailey was created KCMG for his services.

In the lull between Union and the Great War, Sir Abe Bailey withdrew to a great extent from active politics and devoted himself to the Turf in this country, where at Yewhurst, near East Grinstead, he had acquired a fine estate. The troublous year 1914 found Sir Abe at his place in South Africa. In the Boer Rebellion - which signalized South Africa's entry into the War under General Botha - Bailey was quickly in the field as Intelligence Officer to Major-General Sir Henry Lukin. In December 1914, he was attached to General Botha's staff with the rank of major, and took part in the German South-West Africa campaign, as Deputy Assistant Quartermaster-General, 6th Mounted Brigade. In 1919, he was created a baronet.

In 1915, Sir Abe entered the Union Parliament. Standing as an Independent for his old seat at Krugersdorp, in the Transvaal, he maintained that attitude in Parliament, taking his seat among the members of the South African Party behind General Botha, and not, as was hopefully anticipated at the time, among the Unionists, whom he had once served as Whip. In this, "Abe" was not at fault in his prescience of coming events - the absorption of the Unionists in the South African Party and the concentration of their joint forces under the leadership of General Jan Smuts. He retained his seat in the elections of 1920 and 1921, eventually losing it in 1924. But his withdrawal from Parliament in that year implied no failure of interest in South African and Imperial politics, in which he continued to intervene with characteristic speeches and interviews and occasional letters to *The Times*.

The last years of his life were divided about equally between England, where he consistently won laurels on the Turf and took a close interest behind the scenes in politics, and South Africa, where Sir Herbert Baker had built for him a beautiful seaside house at Muizenberg. In both countries - notably at the house in Bryanston Square which was his London home for many years - he entertained magnificently with a generous and genuine hospitality, which made the highest and the humblest alike feel happy and at home under his roof.

Sir Abe Bailey was twice married, first, in 1894, to Caroline, daughter of Mr John Paddon, a well-known merchant of those days in Kimberley. She died in 1902. In 1911, he married the Hon Mary Westenra, daughter of the late Lord Rossmore, and is survived by children of both marriages. He is succeeded by his eldest son, John Milner Bailey, who was born in 1900. Lady Bailey has become famous among airwomen for her long and intrepid flights.

47

ROBERT BOSCH (SEPTEMBER 23, 1861 – MARCH 12, 1942)

THE NEW YORK TIMES, MARCH 13, 1942

*B*erne, Switzerland, March 12 - Dr Robert Bosch, German industrialist and manufacturer of the magneto bearing his name, died at Stuttgart early this morning after an illness of a few days. His age was 81.

Dr Bosch, who opened a small shop half a century ago, became known as a manufacturer and inventor of magnetos, spark plugs, lamps, horns and oil pump devices.

His company had branches all over the world and his German plants employed 25,000 workers before the outbreak of the present war, according to one estimate. In 1906, he introduced the 44-hour week in his factories and his wages were 60 per cent higher than those paid elsewhere. This preceded by eight years the introduction of Henry Ford's $5 minimum scale.

He received his initial technical training in this country when he visited here at the age of 23. Dr Bosch worked with Sigmund Bergmann and Thomas A. Edison, and then went to England, where he was employed at the Siemens works at Woolwich. At the age of 25, he opened his own workshop in Stuttgart, where he made house telephone appliances with two assistants. Upon the suggestion of Gottlieb Daimler, the automobile engineer, he started manufacturing spark plugs.

In 1901, when 50 men worked in his factory, he developed the Bosch magneto and Bosch lamp, which were the foundation of his world-wide reputation.

The first World War and the following period of industrial expansion added to Dr Bosch's fame and fortune. He was opposed to the Reich's imperialistic aims in 1914 and at various times he rebuffed the Kaiser, refusing to accept from him honors and distinctions.

But under the German Republic, he received from President Paul von Hindenburg the Eagle Plaque, and on his seventy-fifth birthday in 1936, which coincided with his fiftieth business anniversary, Nazi Germany acclaimed him as a man whose inventive genius, commercial integrity and enterprise had brought world fame to the fatherland.

German interests in the American Bosch Magneto Corporation were seized during the first World War, and sensational suits arose afterward in German efforts to regain control.

He had three daughters and a son, who died in 1921.

48

LOUIS RENAULT (FEBRUARY 12, 1877 – OCTOBER 24, 1944)

THE NEW YORK TIMES, OCTOBER 25, 1944

*P*aris, October 24 - Louis Renault, pioneer automobile manufacturer, who developed, with his late brother, the largest motor-car plant in France, died this morning in a Paris clinic while under police observation. He was 63 years old.

Mr Renault was arrested on September 23 on a charge of having worked for the enemy, but on account of ill health he was taken to a nursing home instead of jail. His condition became worse and a week ago he was transferred to the surgical clinic. Death resulted from uremia.

The Renault works at Billancourt in the Paris suburbs covered several acres and when operating at full capacity employed as many as 40,000 men. In addition to automobiles, it turned out tractors and various other items of military equipment. In the First World War, the French Army used many Renault light tanks. During the German occupation, Billancourt came under enemy control, with the consequence that it was bombed repeatedly by both the RAF and the American Air Forces. There were many civilian casualties.

For his defense, Mr Renault argued that by continuing operations he prevented unemployment and that in any case the Germans would have attained their ends by requisitioning his plant. Soon after the liberation of Paris, the de Gaulle Government ordered the nationalization of the entire factory.

On June 11, 1940, three days before the Germans entered Paris, Louis Renault was in Washington and called on President Franklin D. Roosevelt, with whom, according to a United Press statement, he "conferred on war material production". On June 23, he left on the Yankee clipper for Lisbon, uncertain of his eventual destination because of conditions in France.

When arrested recently, Mr Renault called attention to this American visit, saying: "At the moment of the armistice, I was in America studying the manufacture of tanks. When I got back to France, I found the factories occupied by the Germans. General Maxime Weygand had ordered production continued. It had to be to prevent workers and machines being sent to Germany."

Later, he asserted that while working for the Germans he restrained production so as to accumulate large stocks of raw material.

In an October 7 dispatch from Paris, Harold Callender wrote in *The New York Times* that: "There are many uneasy consciences here about M. Renault's arrest and the seizure of his properties. For he is said by some business men to have produced as little as possible for the Germans and by producing to have retained his factories intact for French use after liberation."

Fifteen years ago, Mr Renault was one of the strong advocates of a prohibitive French tariff against American automobiles. He said that "snobbery" caused Frenchmen to buy American cars, although French automobiles were superior because they were more durable,

held the road better, and had more effective brakes. This superiority he said had been attained by French manufacturers in the years 1926-29.

If foreign cars were to dominate the French market, he contended, it would not have been worthwhile "to have lost a million and a half men in the war of 1914-18 to escape German tutelage only to fall under that of America."

49

MILTON HERSHEY (SEPTEMBER 13, 1857 – OCTOBER 13, 1945)

THE NEW YORK TIMES, OCTOBER 14, 1945

*H*ershey, Pennsylvania, October 13 — Milton S. Hershey, chocolate manufacturer and philanthropist who left a trust fund now totaling more than $80,000,000 to "The Orphan Hershey Boys of America", died today in Hershey Hospital. His age was 88.

In recent years, Mr Hershey lived quietly in the town which bears his name and continued to play an active part in community affairs. He was a guest at the 1944 National Conference of Governors held at Hershey.

He first sold candy in Philadelphia but went out of business after his horse-drawn wagon was wrecked. Next, he borrowed money and set himself up in caramel-making in New York and failed again. After a similar fate in Chicago, he went to Lancaster, Philadelphia, in 1888 for another try at caramel-making. Fifteen years later, he sold out for $1,000,000.

With that stake, he bought 1,200 acres near his birthplace and founded his chocolate business which eventually expanded into Cuba where sugar was grown, refined and shipped over his own railroads. The Hershey property, with successive expansions, covers 12,000 acres and the plant handles milk produced by 25,000 cows in dairies throughout central Pennsylvania.

The town of Hershey became a show place in Pennsylvania with its resort hotel, four golf courses, big swimming pool, a sports arena seating 8,000, a park of 1,000 acres and a ballroom that has accommodated 4,000 dancers at a time. The town has a population of more than 4,000.

He founded the Hershey Industrial School in 1918 and set up a trust fund of $60,000,000 which has grown to more than $80,000,000. A board of directors handles applications for entrance to the school. With the death of Mr Hershey, direction of the chocolate king's vast enterprise goes to P. A. Staples, a Hershey associate for almost a quarter of a century. Mr Staples joined the Hershey interests in Cuba as president and general manager of the Hershey Corporation. He also has been a director of the corporation for many years.

Mr Hershey's wife, the former Catherine Sweeney, of Jamestown, New York, died in 1915. They had no children.

Milton Snavely Hershey (M.S. to his associates) spent the latter years of his life as a minister without portfolio to the business he had founded and to the town which grew as a natural concomitant. For in 1923, he divested himself of the bulk of his holdings in the Hershey Chocolate Company to provide an endowment of $60,000,000 for the Hershey Industrial School for Orphans. He endowed the school with 500,000 of his 729,000 shares of Hershey common stock.

Hershey, Philadelphia, is a one-industry town, a "company" town, but withal a modern, forward-looking village which might furnish the model for any American planned municipality. This development, which attracts annually more than 60,000 visitors, arose naturally with the growth of the chocolate candy business which Mr Hershey started in the cornfields of his birthplace in 1903. A corollary development was the construction of 267 miles of railroad in Cuba connecting two provinces, and the building of hotels and villages there to care for the workers who operate three sugar mills and the plantations which feed them.

Mr Hershey was born on September 13, 1857, in the house which now serves as headquarters of the Hershey Industrial School, one mile south of Hershey. His parents were Henry H. and Fanny B. Snavely Hershey, both Mennonites. Mrs Hershey was the daughter of a Mennonite bishop.

Mr Hersey attended school in the little red schoolhouse which is now the caddy house of the community club golf course. Then he became a printer's devil on the Lancaster *Waffenlose Waechter*, a paper using both German and English typography. He disliked the job; his straw hat fell into the Press one day and his unpleasant task ceased.

After his first retirement in 1903, he and his wife began a trip around the world. They reached Mexico City, the end of the first stage of the trip. Mr Hershey sat on a hotel porch for a while, enduring leisure. Suddenly, he rose, sought his wife, and announced: "I can't stand this; I've got to get back to work." So back to the United States they came and Mr Hershey pondered on the choice of a new product and a place to manufacture.

He decided to make chocolate, he later explained, because he wanted a candy which would retain the impress of his name in the summer, something the caramels had failed to do.

He started with 12 families of his old workers, planning to enlist other help as needed from the neighbourhood. Even today, Hershey workers do not look like the factory workers of other industries. One sees bonneted women and bearded Amish and Mennonite men coming from the factory doors at night. The workers are mostly of local stock.

The model community which has developed in Hershey came not because of any paternalistic policy by the management but rather because the ramshackle dance halls and amusements which followed a successful and growing business offended Hershey's esthetic and business sense. These places were unsightly and not making money. Mr Hersey took them over.

Until 1909, the chocolate factory had been Mr Hershey's baby. Then, he and Mrs. Hershey being childless, they decided to educate orphan boys. The chocolate factory became secondary; it was the means of providing funds for Mr Hershey's major interest.

Orphan boys between the ages of 4 and 15 are housed at the school in small groups under a house mother, trained in academic, vocational or commercial courses and, when 18, leave the school with a job, clothes to last a year and $100 in addition to any savings from money they may have earned while in school.

The Hershey Industrial School grew so rapidly that in 1934 it became necessary to build an entire group of buildings occupying a space on a high ridge of the foothills of the Blue Ridge Mountains. Boys are admitted, after a physical and psychometric examination, from the three surrounding counties, next the State of Pennsylvania and finally the rest of the country.

In 1936, Mr Hershey formed the M.S. Hershey Foundation, with an endowment of 5,000 shares of Hershey common stock, then worth $400,000, to establish and maintain one or more schools for the education of Derry Township boys and girls after they were graduated from high school. Two years later, the Hershey Junior College for boys and girls was opened.

For creating ration "D", familiar to all servicemen as the "iron ration", the Hershey Chocolate Corporation received the Army-Navy "E" production award in 1942. After his eighty-seventh birthday, Mr Hershey resigned the presidency of three of his corporations, the Hershey Industrial School, the Hershey Corporation and the Hershey Trust Company. He continued as chairman of the board of the Hershey Chocolate Corporation.

Hershey was one community in the United States that was unaware of the depression that began in 1929. For one thing, the unit sale was 5 cents, and accordingly less affected than the sales in businesses where the unit was much larger. But Mr Hershey took positive steps. While the country at large suffered, Hershey had a boom. Mr Hershey picked those years to build homes for workers, a community house, a luxurious hotel, a high school building and other improvements.

This one-man public works program kept the community busy, and aided neighboring areas as well. Mr Hershey had evolved a system dealing with his employees which for a generation kept the plant free from industrial disputes. A quarter of the profits in business were distributed every three months in the form of dividends upon wages and salaries. He improved the livestock of the surrounding counties, but never owned a racing stable.

He traveled abroad much, but never had a yacht. In fact, whenever he traveled, he had to have a cloak of business to cover the trip; a matter of the Italian almond market, or something similar.

The effect of the Hershey community extended out into the countryside like the ripples from a stone tossed into a pool. Early in 1937, the Committee for Industrial Organization established a branch of the United Chocolate Workers of America in Hershey, and in April staged a sit-down strike. The farmers, who for years had sold their milk to the Hershey plant and whose herds had been improved by Hershey sires, routed the strikers with clubs and fists. A Federal Regional Labor Board held an election, and the CIO union was rejected by a vote of 1,542 to 781. The plant thereupon retained its old status of operation.

In 1935, he made one of the last of his philanthropic gestures, contributing $100,000 to the town's five churches, with which they were instructed to pay off their debts. As for personal wealth, Mr Hershey was a man of moderate means, his closest associates said. "He didn't even own the house in which he lived - he gave that away some years ago to his employees for a country club."

HENRY FORD (JULY 30, 1863 – APRIL 7, 1947)

THE MANCHESTER GUARDIAN, APRIL 9, 1947

*H*enry Ford (whose death is announced on page 5) was born at Greenfield, Michigan, in 1863. In his youth, he worked as a mechanic, and had a struggle with poverty. He was for some time in Detroit, in the employ of the Edison Illuminating Company, of which he became chief engineer. He then turned his attention to the making of automobiles, with the object especially of constructing a car so cheap that almost any regular earner of fair wages could afford one.

When, in 1901, he finished the first good four-cycle engine ever built and mounted it on his old car of discarded bicycle wheels and boards for a midnight run, it marked the culmination of 13 years of steady labour.

In 1903, he organised the Ford Motor Company, with a capital of $100,000. In that year, it employed 311 men and its total output was 1,708 cars. By 1917, there were 41,000 men in his factories, with a daily output of 3,000 motor-cars and motor-wagons, and he was paying super-tax on an income of $35,000,000 a year. The Ford product soon became famous throughout America as the car "which makes walking a luxury", and in no long time it gained a great vogue among persons in all other countries who required a comparatively inexpensive machine.

Indirectly, it contributed largely to the rapid spread of the Non-Partisan League in the Middle West, for the farmers who organised that movement were enabled, by means of their Ford cars, to meet for common political action as it would have been impossible for them to do otherwise. The development of his enterprise led to the setting up of works at Trafford Park, Manchester, and in Cork, and still later at Dagenham.

In 1914, Ford shocked the American industrial world by announcing a plan of profit-sharing which involved the distribution of $10,000,000 a year to his employees. He made it known at the same time that hereafter the minimum wage in his factories would be five dollars a day, this rule applying even to the boys who swept the floors and ran errands. He supplemented the regular wage with a bonus of two dollars for workers who kept their homes clean and sanitary, and did not fill their beds with lodgers. He maintained a corps of social workers to look after the welfare of his employees and their families and provided also medical and legal departments free of charge.

Ford essayed a new role early in December 1915. When he chartered the liner Oscar II as a peace ship, taking out a party of peace advocates who were to "get the boys out of the trenches before Christmas" by influencing the belligerent Governments to end the war. This modern example of knight errantry stirred the imagination, but effected nothing. In the following year, Ford received several votes at the first ballot for the Presidential nomination at the Republican National Convention, and in 1918 he was defeated by a very small margin as a candidate for the United States Senate.

A more serious movement towards placing him in high political office took place in 1923, in prospect of the 1924 election. Nothing came of it in the end, but at one time the Ford "boom" for the Presidency reached such proportions as to perplex and alarm the professional politicians. A "straw vote", taken by a weekly paper, which placed him well ahead of any other candidate was, at any rate, a striking evidence of his national popularity.

In 1921, he surprised even his warmest admirers and almost staggered Wall Street by the financial skill by which he saved his great organisation at a critical moment when it had to face maturing obligations amounting to $750,000,000. The story has often been told of how the emissary of a group of confident bankers laid before him a plan for reorganisation which would enable him to meet these obligations, but would place him completely at the mercy of his "rescuers", and of how at the end of a brief interview the visitor was politely shown the door.

During the following years, Ford, so far from contracting his activities, enlarged them, becoming the owner of extensive coal lands, iron mines, blast furnaces, steel mills, forests, canals, railroads, and water-power plants, to say nothing of *The Dearborn Independent*, a weekly paper carrying no advertisements and boasting a circulation of 650,000 copies. In 1924, there was sharp controversy in both Houses of Congress over his bid for the vast power project at Muscle Shoals. He offered $5,000,000 for the physical property and a total of $219,000,000 payable during 100 years for leases on the hydroelectric power plants.

President Roosevelt's "New Deal" aroused Ford's vehement hostility. Alone among American automobile manufacturers, he refused in 1933 to sign the code drawn up by the National Recovery Administration for the regulation of the motor industry. At the same time, he raised the wages of many of his employees and reduced their hours of work; thus, it was remarked, living up to the spirit of the code while ignoring the letter.

In 1935, however, the Act conferring code-making powers on the NRA was declared unconstitutional by the Supreme Court. In 1937, the National Labour Relations Board investigated charges brought by the labour unions against the Ford Company and pronounced it to have been guilty of "utter recklessness and savage anti-union activity". The Board ordered the reinstatement of men who had been dismissed for union activities, and instructed the company to end the organisation of its private union (the Ford Brotherhood of America) and to cease its intimidation of labour organisations.

When the Second World War broke out, Ford maintained for a time the pacifist attitude for which he had been conspicuous in 1915. He refused, for instance, to make Rolls-Royce engines, of which two-thirds of the output was to go to the British. He supported Wendell Willkie, however, at the 1940 election, although Willkie was in favour of all aid to Britain. In January 1941, Ford showed himself willing to cooperate in the defence of his own country, but despite the lowness of his tender, the United States War Department refused to allocate a $12,500,000 contract to him on the ground of his non-observance of the Federal labour laws.

Within a few months, the policy of hostility to unionism in which Ford had persisted throughout his career came to an abrupt and sensational end. In April 1941, a strike, lasting for 10 days, shut down a Ford plant and tied up $155,000,000 in defence contracts. It ended by the company's signing an agreement with the CIO's United Automobile Workers of America. This contract, affecting about 130,000 employees, not only included a wages and hours agreement but turned the Ford works into a "union shop", in which the workmen's dues were to be collected by the company itself.

In 1941, Ford and his son Edsel (who died in 1943) gave a fleet of 350 specially constructed and equipped food vans, valued at over £150,000, for the benefit of victims of air raids in Great Britain.

When the United States became a belligerent, Ford gave himself wholeheartedly to the war effort. He established at Willow Run, near Detroit, a vast aircraft-production factory which, by the ingenuity of its methods and the vast scale of its operations, astounded every visitor. Incidentally, he built, at a cost of $625,000, a school to train workers, already familiar with the production of motors, for the more complicated mechanism of bombers.

In 1943, on the death of his son Edsel, Ford resumed the presidency of the Ford Motor Company, which he had relinquished to Edsel 25 years before. He resigned it again in September 1945, handing over to his 28-year-old grandson, Henry Ford.

There is, of course, no exact or verifiable knowledge of the extent of Ford's fortune, but he is generally supposed to have been the wealthiest of all the American millionaires. In 1927, Mr Stuart Chase, the distinguished American economist, published an estimate which gave the joint fortune of Henry Ford and his son Edsel as $1,200,000,000, the Rockefellers, father and son, coming next with precisely half that sum

Though one of the wealthiest men in America, Mr Ford lived in the simplest style, occupying with his wife a modest bungalow on his 2,000-acre farm and employing only two servants in his household. His principal hobby was natural history, especially the observation of the habits and ways of life of wild birds. He was assisted in this study by John Burroughs, who was one of his dearest friends.

Ford expounded his industrial and social philosophy in several volumes, some of them written in collaboration with Mr Samuel Crowther. Their titles are *My Life and Work*, *Today and Tomorrow*, *My Philosophy of Industry* and *Moving Forward*. The outstanding tenet of "Detroitism", as Mr Ramsay Muir called his creed, is the belief in mass production, with which is coupled the theory that high wages, high production, and high consumption go together. The Ford doctrine won thousands of adherents both in the United States and abroad, but the depression of 1929 turned many of them into sceptics, even - or, perhaps, especially - at Detroit itself, which did not escape the pinch of hard times more than any other American industrial centre. Mr André Siegfried found in this doctrine the essential expression of modern Americanism, and, contrasting it with Oriental ideals, closed his illuminating study *America Comes of Age* with the significant sentence, "The discussion broadens until it becomes, as it were, a dialogue between Ford and Gandhi."

The New York Times, April 9, 1947

He was a simple, in some ways almost naïve, man, and it was in the quality of logical directness perhaps that his chief genius lay. To a peculiar degree, he was the embodiment of America in the era of industrial revolution. Starting as a Midwestern farm boy, he became a mechanic, went into business for himself, and was finally one of the wealthiest men. It was the American success story. The world was horse-drawn when he entered it. When he departed, it was a world on powered wheels. He was a pacifist, and yet it was the tremendous impact of his pioneering and development of the mass-production technique that, when multiplied by the hundredfold throughout the country, made us supreme over the enemy in war. For without that conveyor belt, we could never have become the arsenal of democracy, in guns, planes, ships and other vehicles of war that spelled victory. And without that same assembly line, labor, which often denounced Henry Ford, would not have enjoyed the same high standard of living that it has through quantity production.

The Scotsman, April 9, 1947

FORD'S LIFE LENDS WEIGHT to the old adage that genius is born and not made. His work, however, cannot be explained solely in terms of innate ability. He himself has said that "More men are beaten than fail. It is not just wisdom they need or money or brilliance, but just plain gristle and bone." This view rather bears out Carlyle's dictum that genius consists in a transcendent capacity for taking trouble. Ford knew what his calling was in life, and he was determined to follow it. The efforts of his father to settle him on a farm; the meagre wages and long hours of his first engineering job in Detroit; the vicissitudes of his early attempts to manufacture cars; and the jibes of his colleagues - none of these could deflect him from his firm resolve. He earned success not only by his brilliance but by his grit and staying power. At times, he was the only one who believed in himself, but he never lost that belief. He gave the world the cheap motor car; but he did much more. He gave it an idea, and that - the technique of the assembly unit - is the basis of mass production.

Yet these - his contributions to the evolution of transport

and of mass production - do not exhaust his claims to greatness. The efficiency of his factories, coupled with the high wages of his workmen, gave a lesson to labour as well as to capital. While in promoting the welfare of his employees he sought to be ahead of his competitors - and his success here has been recognised in Trade Union circles in the USA despite his opposition to Trade Unionism - his workers realised that this was not feasible without loyal co-operation on their part. It is this lesson - the relationship between joint product and joint effort - that British labour needs to be reminded of today. Although on certain prominent issues Henry Ford expressed views which were far from popular, throughout he was actuated by intense humanism, and his passing will be deeply felt throughout the world.

The Marion Star, Ohio, April 8, 1947

JUST AS HE HAD MANY SUCCESSES, so, too, did he experience many defeats, but Ford rarely appeared disturbed. He abhorred court suits that required personal appearances. There was the million dollar libel suit Ford brought against the *Chicago Tribune* in 1919 for calling him an anarchist. The six-cent verdict he won was a bitter victory, for he underwent a grilling on the witness stand that probably marked a new high point for searching questions in an attempt to impeach his intelligence.

Ford was defeated in 1918 for United States senator by a narrow margin. He settled out of court in 1927 a suit brought against him by Aaron Sapiro, Chicago attorney and promoter of farmers' cooperatives. The suit grew from the anti-Jewish campaign conducted in Ford's weekly newspaper, *The Dearborn Independent*. This paper was discontinued shortly after the suit was settled. A disappointment rather than a failure was Ford's unsuccessful effort in 1926 to purchase the government's Muscle Shoals property in Alabama. He had ambitious plans for the development of the property both in water power and nitrate production, but his offer was declined after months of acrimonious debate in congress.

Henry Ford was born on a farm in Greenfield township, Michigan, a suburb of Detroit on July 30, 1863. His father, William Ford, was an Irish immigrant; his mother, Mary Litogot, was of Dutch ancestry. Her parents owned land adjoining the Ford farm. Ford had three sisters and two brothers, all younger than himself. Contrary to popular belief, Ford was not the son of impoverished parents. His father was well-to-do as a farmer, and when Henry married his parents offered him a farm of his own in the vicinity. Young Ford, however, had visions of a career in mechanics. It is somewhat paradoxical that, although he disliked the farm in early life, he went back to it in a large way after an industrial career had brought him enormous wealth. His return to farming, however, was to promote his conviction that agriculture and industry needed each other.

39667619R00159

Printed in Poland
by Amazon Fulfillment
Poland Sp. z o.o., Wrocław